Six Sigma for
Business Excellence

Six Sigma for Business Excellence

A Manager's Guide to Supervising Six Sigma Projects and Teams

Penelope Przekop

Penelope Przekop (signature)

McGraw-Hill

New York Chicago San Francisco Lisbon
London Madrid Mexico City Milan New Delhi
San Juan Seoul Singapore Sydney Toronto

The McGraw·Hill Companies

1 2 3 4 5 6 7 8 9 0 DOC/DOC 0 9 8 7 6 5

ISBN 0-07-144809-8

This publication is designed to provide accurate and authoritative information in
regard to the subject matter covered. It is sold with the understanding that the
publisher is not engaged in rendering legal, accounting, or other professional service. If legal advice or other expert assistance is required, the services of a competent professional person should be sought.
> —*From a declaration of principles jointly adopted by a committee of the
> American Bar Association and a committee of publishers.*

McGraw-Hill books are available at special quantity discounts to use as premiums
and sales promotions, or for use in corporate training programs. For more information, please write to the Director of Special Sales, McGraw-Hill Professional,
Two Penn Plaza, New York, NY 10121-2298. Or contact your local bookstore.

 This book is printed on recycled, acid-free paper containing a
minimum of 50% recycled, de-inked fiber.

Contents

Preface

You should see my to-do list. It symbolizes all the responsibility I once dreamed of having. It's beautiful, but like a rose it has thorns that sometimes prevent me from enjoying it as much as I'd like to. And it's a vine, growing around every office supply my company bought for me, through every file drawer packed with proposals and presentations I've developed, and across every organized pile I've created.

As a director at Johnson & Johnson, I manage a staff of professionals who are responsible for a lot of important stuff. Day-to-day, I focus on my deliverables (they're written down in numerous places in my office), but I can't ignore all the e-mail I get (an average of 100 a day). If I don't respond to those that are directly addressed to me, a negative perception will grow as fast as my to-do list. As all my responses are in writing, they need to be correct—words that I can stand behind tomorrow or next year. I'll admit that I'm trying to climb the corporate ladder. I watch everyone else, trying to learn from the successes and mistakes of my peers and my mentors. I'm trying to bring in the additional staff that I finally got approved and spend time each day with the staff outside my office door.

Enter the traditional Six Sigma project.

Of course, I'm all for quality and cost savings, efficiency, and improvement, but my plate is full. And I'm so close to implementing the great ideas I have based on proven experience. I just need to get my Admin to schedule those interviews. I'm trying to call the Admin when the first e-mail pops onto my computer screen. It's from the Six Sigma project Black Belt. She's professional and polished. She dresses for success. Her presentation at the kick-off meeting was extremely impressive, overflowing with Six Sigma language and methodology, not to mention the concepts I've spent my career trying to instill upon others as a quality management professional. But I wondered if my peers were following her. I wondered if she was too impressive, too methodical. She made me feel enthusiastic, but some of my colleagues looked exhausted and even bored by the end of the three-hour meeting. A few seemed to be thinking about the to-do lists and e-mails awaiting them back at the office.

The Black Belt's e-mail says I'm required to complete a Project Charter by the end of the week. It must include the business case and metrics. I should touch base with the other subteam leaders to make sure all the subteam charters are coordinated. I must choose the members of my subteam and make sure they can review the charter before I forward it to her. This may require a meeting. But wait, the focus of my subteam is to determine how we can improve our processes for tracking compliance with regulatory timelines. I already know how to do that. I already have a plan—I just need to get those interviews scheduled.

Give me a break, I say to myself. I don't need a special project to get this done. Another e-mail comes. It says that I should also remember to fill out the Microsoft project template by next Wednesday—our project has extremely tight timelines. Someone knocks at my office door. Five more e-mails pop onto the screen, two of which are marked urgent. I groan, but not too loudly. I always strive to be positive.

Welcome to my world. I am middle management.

The purpose of this book is to explain how middle management can apply the underlying concepts embodied in the Six Sigma movement to our world, regardless of whether the company has committed to Six Sigma or not. It explains how this can be achieved in a way that makes sense for us, that allows the concepts to blend with our everyday goals and responsibilities to achieve outstanding results. And once we embrace the concepts of Six Sigma, we can work with Six Sigma professionals more efficiently. If they come knocking, we can truly share the same goals and speak the same language, regardless of what industry we work in or what function our personal organization serves.

Everything we've heard about Six Sigma screams to us that we must have high-level support or it will fail.

I don't believe that. There, I said it.

They never said that *we* would fail.

They said *it* would fail.

So let's redefine *it*.

Acknowledgments

I would like to acknowledge Ellen Kurtz, Vicki O'Neil, Mary Lou Zett, Lisa Anne Markel, and Janice Bush. You have all contributed to this book through your excellent mentoring at various stages in my career. I would like to thank the Department of Engineering and Technology Management at Southern Polytechnic State University in Marietta, Georgia. Many thanks to my editor, Jeanne Glasser. You took a chance and never wavered in your strong support, patience, and cheerleading. Marcia Layton Turner, thank you for your wonderful, collaborative work on the case studies. To my husband and greatest teacher, Mark, thank you for supporting me always and for putting up with all my late nights at the computer. Thanks to my beautiful daughters, Phoebe and Valerie, for eating cereal for dinner many a night and for listening to me talk about quality management. I would like to thank my mother, Jane Haden, for the undying spark of creatively that you gave me—if only it could shine as brightly as yours. To my father, Bill Hall, I dedicate this book because you instilled in me a love for the written word and always told me that I could achieve my dreams.

Introduction

In 2000, then Johnson & Johnson (J&J) Chairman and CEO Ralph Larsen put process excellence at the top of the multibillion-dollar firm's list of priorities, citing savings of over $5 billion as a result of these efforts in the last several years. J&J's current Chairman Bill Weldon has taken the initiative a step further. Making it clear that process excellence is not an option, Weldon announced that the company "will be the best and most competitive healthcare company in the world and sustain that position through Process Excellence with the use of its assessment and improvement methodologies. This company will never rest in its pursuit of excellence."

To achieve this goal, J&J has created a strong quality environment rooted in Six Sigma that applies to all of their businesses. The J&J approach focuses on assessment, improvement, and recognition. The assessment aspect is firmly rooted in Malcolm Baldrige Criteria for Performance Excellence, and the improvement aspect utilizes key quality concepts and tools from Six Sigma, Lean Thinking, and Design Excellence. Drawing from J&J's use of Six Sigma throughout their pharmaceutical division, *Six Sigma for Business Excellence* will give managers the concepts and tools needed to recreate J&J's approach in their own firms.

But this book is not *specifically* about J&J, GE, Toyota, or any of the big corporations with high-level support for Six Sigma. It's about middle managers across industries, companies, and functions. We are increasingly busy. We are the layer of management who *implement* change. We are also often the group who propose change. Senior management can't quite put its finger on issues easily identified by our knowing eyes. We connect the dots provided by those who report to us when they don't yet have the knowledge and experience to do so themselves. But the majority of us don't have Six Sigma Black Belts. Many of us don't know how to get one, can't get one, or simply have other priorities. But high-level support is critical for successful implementation of Six Sigma. As middle managers, we hear this message at nearly every quality or business conference we attend. We read it in the current business literature. We attend those conferences and read the books because we care about quality and want to make a difference. Each presentation we see and each Six Sigma book we read convinces us that Six Sigma is the answer to true customer satisfaction and an increase in the bottom line. Yet we are bogged down by the overwhelming assignment of convincing senior management, including our CEOs, to champion the companywide culture change needed to spark the Six Sigma revolution; we must have high-level support or it will fail.

The same quality gurus that tell us we need high-level support insist at every turn that quality should not be a program, a special initiative, or a province of the elite. Intuitively, this makes sense. Let's face it; if you're a manager who doesn't particularly care about quality, you shouldn't be a manager. Despite this, far more attention has been placed on gaining senior management support than on how middle managers can actually implement Six Sigma concepts within their own scope of work. In reality, middle managers have two options. We can gain high-level support for implementation of Six Sigma concepts or we can implement the concepts at our level. Realistically, more times than not, middle managers cannot *easily* convince the senior management of their broader organization—much less the CEO—to implement such a huge undertaking. Some middle managers are hard pressed to get a meeting with the decision makers.

Welcome to the world of middle management.

It is time to dispel the myth that middle management is helpless without high-level support. We can, in fact, infuse Six Sigma concepts into our world. The first step in achieving this goal is to begin thinking about managing quality from a more personal perspective. Let's forget about the *entire* company for a while and focus on *our* responsibilities, *our* scope. We must strive to bring Six Sigma into the trenches where the work is done, the ideas are born, and the bottom line is supported.

There are great books available to explain Six Sigma on our level. Most of these books assume that our organization already has high-level support and that we are trying to understand our place in the change. They are kindly assisting our Black Belts with change management. They convince us to join the cause, to work cooperatively with the assigned Six Sigma Black Belt. The terminology is explained; the buzzwords of the day are laid out for us to practice and insert into our repertoire of business expression. Of course, that's useful information if your company has, in fact, decided to implement Six Sigma. In that case, please don't resist. Learn what you can.

The truth is that the concepts at the heart of Six Sigma and most other quality philosophies can be applied to any scope of work—from the smallest to the largest. They can be applied if you manage only yourself or oversee 50. This is your organization. Choose how you will manage it.

This book will describe a self-directed program that managers can use to apply Six Sigma concepts and techniques immediately, without having to enlist high-level support within the organization. Managers at all levels will learn how to improve performance through Six Sigma concepts and tools and thereby incorporate applications more intrinsically into their world. This begins with establishing a personal management framework based on Six Sigma concepts. By doing so, over time, quality can improve from the inside out rather than from the outside in (e.g., through consultants, Black Belts, etc.). Then, if upper management gets the message and starts a formal Six Sigma program, you'll be able to collaborate more effectively with the Black Belts.

The key purpose of this book is to provide functional managers across industries with information, specific tips, and tools for utilizing Six Sigma. In addition, functional managers and Six Sigma professionals will both gain insight into how the other thinks, what their priorities are, and why. After completing this book, both will have a list of specific actions for improved communication.

The book is organized into four parts: a manager's summary that provides the basic information middle managers will need as they champion their own Six Sigma projects; a manager's perspective that aligns Six Sigma operations with the strategic goals of the manager; and an up-close look at a Six Sigma operation from the Black Belt's perspective that will help readers understand the goals and responsibilities of both managers and Six Sigma professionals. The final section explores issues that face both the manager and the Six Sigma professional when their worlds collide.

In Chapter 1, readers will gain an understanding of the underlying quality concepts that drive Six Sigma success. It includes a look at some of the other better known quality management (QM) systems and philosophies such as ISO 9000 and Baldrige Criteria. You will gain an appreciation for the common themes and concepts running through the QM systems and philosophies that are discussed and also gain an understanding of how they relate to overall management of an organization regardless of size or complexity. The common concepts include process focus, customer focus and collaboration, data driven management, and strategic planning. The DMAIC (define, measure, analyze, improve, and control) approach will also be covered as it serves as the foundation for use of the Six Sigma tools.

Once you understand the common themes in Six Sigma thinking and how they relate to management in general, you will be introduced to some of the more common Six Sigma tools in Chapter 2, including Project Charters, Voice of the Customer (VOC) methods, SIPOC (suppliers, inputs, process, outputs, and customers) Diagrams, Pareto Analysis, Control Charts, Impact/Effort Matrix,

Flowcharting, and Sampling. The discussion on Six Sigma tools will begin with the DMAIC approach and explain how and why it calls for use of the tools.

Chapter 3 brings the concepts and tools together in a discussion of how the application of both can provide a tremendous advantage to managers on several levels. This includes advantages for the organization as a whole, for your team, and for yourself on a professional level.

Chapters 4 through 8 explain how managers can apply Six Sigma principles and methods to meet particular business needs. Chapter 4 explains what a management framework is and why it is a key contributor to your long-term success, particularly if your goal is to reach high personal potential and have an impact on your organization.

In Chapter 5, managers will learn how a process focus can positively affect overall effectiveness and efficiency regardless of scope. The chapter will focus on how to identify key processes, external and internal customers, and key deliverables through SIPOC Analysis. Tools and tips to assist in documenting and evaluating processes will be provided and explained. Last, it will include a tutorial on the development of Standard Operating Procedures (SOPs) and the impact they have had on the pharmaceutical industry. This will also include SOP templates and general guidelines to follow when analyzing processes and creating SOPs.

Having identified key processes and customers, Chapter 6 will provide background, concepts, and examples of how a powerful customer focus can impact the manager's scope of work as well as the organization as a whole. Methods for obtaining and understanding the voice of the customer will be described. Tips and suggestions that will help drive a more customer-focused approach through the manager's interactions (as well as the team's) will be provided.

Armed with a clear understanding of key processes and customer needs, managers can begin to identify critical data that will be key to their decision making, as well as their understanding of customer satisfaction, and, thus, quality. Chapter 7 will address basic Six Sigma tools such as Data Collection Plans, Control Charts, and Metric Dashboards relative to the efficiency of their use by the manager. The chapter will stress that the data or metrics generated must be valuable to the customers and your senior management.

The concepts and tools discussed in Chapters 1–7 will become the basic cornerstones or framework with which managers can build a strategy for achieving their quality goals. Chapter 8 will stress that this framework is actually just plain smart management. The idea of leadership management will be introduced.

Chapter 9 will lead the functional manager into the 3,000-foot view of the Six Sigma Black Belt. It will provide background on the who, what, why, where, and how behind the rise of the quality professional in the Six Sigma landscape, with particular focus on pharmaceuticals. Traditional Six Sigma, exemplified by the J&J Process Excellence philosophy, will be explored to provide distinct examples of quality professionals, their approach, and views on how their assigned tasks and responsibilities impact the organization.

Once you understand how an organization rooted in Six Sigma concepts functions, the discussion will move to true examples of their impact. Chapter 10 will include examples from the manufacturing industry. The examples will be provided in a style that speaks to the manager's perspective. Areas and concepts that can easily be applied in day-to-day activities, regardless of scope, will be highlighted. The examples will tie back to the concepts outlined earlier in the book. Chapter 11 will include nonmanufacturing (or service) examples in the same perspective as Chapter 10.

Chapter 12 will shift from examples of Six Sigma projects to issues that face both you and the Six Sigma or quality professional when your worlds collide. It will take an honest look at some of the issues and barriers faced by both when they come together to solve a problem in the organization. Communication will be specifically addressed. The chapter will include examples, comments, and testimonials from quality professionals, as well as tips on how to improve communication. The information will be provided in a positive way, giving an insightful look into the motivations and belief systems of both groups.

After addressing communications issues and how they can best be overcome, managers will begin to gain an understanding of the goals of the quality professional. Chapter 13 will challenge managers to explore their goals honestly. It will provide tips on how the functional manager and the Six Sigma professional can identify and understand common goals and harness that understanding to create the best environment for success.

The book's conclusion will challenge industry to create new and creative avenues to benefit from quality professionals and also to begin to drive quality through the organization from the bottom up. Although quality and culture are driven from the top down, the impact of the individual manager cannot be ignored. Six Sigma concepts can be applied in the day-to-day work. If the philosophy is perpetuated throughout the organization in a way that speaks to managers and makes sense, quality professionals will reap the rewards.

We cannot manage what we do not understand. This holds true for management of people, projects, and processes. Many managers believe that they can be successful, that they have gained the right to manage, based on their keen technical knowledge. However, it takes much more than an excellent understanding of regulations, a particular product, or the intricate details of specialized equipment to rise above the management crowd. Managers at all levels who move ahead end up with topnotch CVs and consistently please senior management by striving to understand the motivations of those whom they manage, the specific needs of their customers, and the processes that ultimately provide these people satisfaction.

In his book, *The Six Sigma Way*, Peter Pande tells us that a real Six Sigma organization is one that has taken up the challenge of measuring and improving *all* processes, with the objective of creating a culture of continuous improvement. Simply using Six Sigma measures or a few tools does not qualify a company to be a "Six Sigma Organization." However, if you and your direct reports are an "organization," Six Sigma concepts and tools can be incorporated into your management framework. As managers, we are faced with the task of managing, whether it is people or projects. In the end, there must be an outcome, an output that we are responsible for passing to the next fellow or group or organization. Let's begin to take the responsibility rather than wait for high-level support. The following chapters explore the underlying concepts that have contributed to the remarkable success of organizations like J&J, GE, and Toyota.

Six Sigma for
Business Excellence

Part One

Inside Six Sigma: A Manager's Summary

Chapter 1

Understanding the Key Concepts of Six Sigma

Common sense is not so common.

—Voltaire

Johnson & Johnson is the world's most comprehensive and broadly based manufacturer of health care products, as well as a provider of related services for the consumer, pharmaceutical, medical, and diagnostic markets. The corporation achieved this leadership by concentrating on a unique form of decentralized management, following the ethical principals embodied in the J&J Credo, which follows, and managing the business for the long term.

J&J was founded in 1886 as a supplier of healthcare products. It now has more than 200 operating companies in 57 countries, selling products throughout the world. In 2003, J&J sales were $41.9 billion. J&J has approximately 110,600 employees worldwide and has extensive worldwide research and supply chain capabilities.

In 2004:

- According to an annual corporate reputation survey conducted by Harris Interactive and the Reputation Institute, J&J was acknowledged for having the best corporate reputation in American for the fifth consecutive year.
- J&J tied for first place in *Chief Executive*'s annual ranking of the Top 20 Companies for Leaders.
- J&J was named Number 4 on *Fortune*'s annual list of Global Most Admired Companies. J&J ranked Number 7 on the magazine's list of American's Most Admired Companies and ranked as the Number 1 company in the survey's pharmaceuticals category.

3

Our Credo

We believe our first responsibility is to the doctors, nurses, and patients,
to mothers and fathers and all others who use our products and services.
In meeting their needs everything we do must be of high quality.

We must constantly strive to reduce our costs
in order to maintain reasonable prices.

Customers' orders must be serviced promptly and accurately.

Our suppliers and distributors must have an opportunity
to make a fair profit.

We are responsible to our employees,
the men and women who work with us throughout the world.

Everyone must be considered as an individual.

We must respect their dignity and recognize their merit.

They must have a sense of security in their jobs.

Compensation must be fair and adequate,
and working conditions clean, orderly, and safe.

We must be mindful of ways to help our employees fulfill
their family responsibilities.

Employees must feel free to make suggestions and complaints.

There must be equal opportunity for employment, development,
and advancement for those qualified.

We must provide competent management,

and their actions must be just and ethical.

We are responsible to the communities in which we live and work
and to the world community as well.

We must be good citizens—support good works and charities
and bear our fair share of taxes.

We must encourage civic improvements and better health and education.

We must maintain in good order
the property we are privileged to use,
protecting the environment and natural resources.

Our final responsibility is to our stockholders.

Business must make a sound profit.

We must experiment with new ideas.

Research must be carried on, innovative programs developed,
and mistakes paid for.

New equipment must be purchased, new facilities provided,
and new products launched.

Reserves must be created to provide for adverse times.

When we operate according to these principles,

the stockholders should realize a fair return.

- J&J was ranked Number 16 in *Forbes*'s April 2004 article on power brands, an examination of the intangible assets of reputation, innovation, management, and human capital.
- J&J was ranked Number 24 in *Business Week*'s 50, an annual listing of the top-performing companies.
- J&J was ranked Number 30 in *Fortune*'s list of the 500 largest U.S. corporations.

The long-term success of J&J can be attributed to many factors, including its Credo values, strong long-term leadership, decentralized structure, and innovation. However, J&J has maintained a strong focus on quality, particularly since the 1920s when standard work practices took root in U.S. industry. By the 1930s and throughout the 1940s, J&J began to institute formal improvement programs. In the 1980s, J&J developed a formal Quality Improvement Process and established a Corporate Quality Institute. In the 1990s, J&J implemented its Signature of Quality (SOQ) assessment system based on the Malcolm Baldrige Criteria for Performance Excellence established by the U.S. Congress in 1987. In addition, in the 1990s, the J&J Quality Management Group was established.

In 1995, J&J went through a time of reengineering. The J&J marketplace was changing and it needed to reengineer by looking at the processes that delivered value to customers. By 1997, J&J completed a major benchmarking project in which 200 companies were examined—internal and external, national and global. Based on the ongoing reengineering efforts, the benchmarking results, and the changing marketplace, J&J Process Excellence was born to initiate a critical business imperative to drive business improvement.

J&J designed a system that united what it found to be the best practices. Six Sigma was teamed with Lean Thinking, Design Excellence concepts, and their existing Signature of Quality Assessment Program to form J&J Process Excellence. The first project to utilize Six Sigma methodology took place at Ortho Biotech. After years of failure to increase yield for one of their key products, the use of Six Sigma methodology resulted in a 66 percent increase in yield in four months. This translated to an annualized cost improvement of $17 million and revenue improvement of $500 million.

J&J Process Excellence was officially launched in 1999 in the United States and parts of Europe. In 2001, J&J's then CEO, Ralph Larson, included the following passage regarding Process Excellence in the J&J Annual Report.

From the J&J 2001 Annual Report

The second management imperative (of J&J) is Process Excellence. It is an extension of the Signature of Quality (SOQ) initiative, which for the past several years has been an important part of our worldwide drive for continuous improvement. Process Excellence consolidates all of our learning into a proven and high-powered methodology that incorporates such concepts as Six Sigma, Design Excellence, and quick robust Lean Thinking.

While our Company is highly decentralized and we pride ourselves on giving our management a great deal of running room, Process Excellence is not optional. It is a process that we have made mandatory throughout the entire company. It is nothing less than the application of martial arts training and discipline. It starts with rigorous training in statistical analysis and problem solving techniques, and it includes developing metrics and dashboard measurements for virtually any process in the organization.

SOQ Process Excellence is not simply a cost reduction effort, although it surely does reduce costs. The implementation of Process Excellence has been an important contributor to the productivity efforts that have helped us to take almost $5 billion in costs out of the Company over the past five years. To put it another way, that means our annual operating costs today are $5 billion lower…and we believe we have just scratched the surface.

Perhaps the biggest payoff from Process Excellence is that it helps to drive growth. It reduces the time required to develop new products and it gives us greater confidence in the efficacy of our new products. We are convinced that Process Excellence makes us a more formidable competitor at every level, and it drives both volume and profits.

> Six Sigma is the chosen improvement methodology used by Johnson & Johnson to attack process variability in order to eliminate defects. Johnson & Johnson Process Excellence (PE) follows the DMAIIC Roadmap:
>
> Define—gain agreement on scope & project purpose
>
> Measure—gather baseline data
>
> Analyze—determine root causes
>
> Innovate/Improve—pilot & implement solutions
>
> Control—sustain improvement gains

Six Sigma as a Corporate Mission

Johnson & Johnson determined that the DMAIC cycle, with the addition of "innovate," could provide a strategy and framework on which to build a Process Excellence organization. Before J&J began using Six Sigma, Motorola and GE were the middle manager's initial examples of Six Sigma success. The CEOs of these corporations made Six Sigma a top priority and pushed the methodology down through the organization. They established Six Sigma as the management framework by which their organizations would run. Employees were encouraged or required to take Six Sigma Champion, Black Belt, and Green Belt training. They were expected to produce results based on Six Sigma projects. Books were written to not only explain Six Sigma, but also to tell management how these organizations underwent the Six Sigma transformation. It was impressive.

As the word spread, Six Sigma methodology began popping up at various business and quality conferences. Soon entire conferences were created around the Six Sigma way. Everyone interested wanted to understand how to apply the pre-scribed methodology. Many middle managers became interested in how they could create the changes seen in these early examples but were told that extremely high-level support is needed to create a Six Sigma organization similar to that of GE, Motorola, and Toyota. If middle managers could convince CEOs to join the cause, they stood the best chance for transformation. Without this high-level support, efforts will fail. Good luck!

To create another GE, staunch CEO commitment is needed. We can accept that. This makes sense. What does not make sense is the notion that the underlying concepts of Six Sigma cannot be implemented without high-level support, that efforts will fail before they begin. Middle managers can create Six Sigma organizations in their own backyards. The basic ingredients are there:

- Processes
- Customers
- Suppliers
- People
- Ideas
- Technical expertise
- Commitment to quality

Six Sigma can be championed at middle-management levels if we choose to take Six Sigma to a more personal level.

In order to fully appreciate the underlying concepts of Six Sigma, an understanding of the basic principles of quality management is needed. Six Sigma, ISO 9000, and the Malcolm Baldrige Criteria for Performance Excellence are some of the better-known quality management systems or philosophies that have evolved from the study of quality as a science. People who are particularly interested in quality (as a science), including the Japanese who rose to quality power after World War II, have intently studied these principles over time. The Japanese were able to create a culture where each manager, or even individual, is personally committed to quality. In contrast, we have a culture where each person feels entitled to be the recipient of quality. But who among us produces quality products and services day to day? This tends to happen at the middle management level as opposed to those in the C-suite.

Quality Management Systems

A *quality management (QM) system* is a tool used by management that is designed to ensure product quality and customer satisfaction. A system is the organizational structure, responsibilities, procedures, and resources needed to conduct a major function within a business or to support a common business need. Systems are usually made up of many major processes that take an input, add value to it, and produce an output. Quality management systems are primarily used by manufacturers, but they are also used in nonmanufacturing businesses such as hotels, banks, and insurance companies. In general, one measures the quality of a product or service by seeking to determine if it has met the intended need of the customer. This could be a need that was stated up front, before the product was designed, or it could be a perceived customer need that is being met, such as with new products and services that are offered based on market research data or some other means of defining general customer needs or desires. (This is actually just smart business practice.)

Depending on the complexity of the product or service, numerous steps or tasks must be performed appropriately to ensure that the final product or service turns out as intended. Companies sometimes institute a QM system to ensure that all the necessary steps or tasks are being carried out. This helps the company ensure that the product or service will be delivered as planned and helps identify as early as possible in the process when something goes wrong. The QM system can include documentation, quality checks, statistical methods to evaluate data obtained throughout the process, and methods to ensure that corrections are made when needed.

Some industries, such as the automotive industry, have adopted specific QM systems that are generally used industry-wide. This allows for consistency among manufacturers, which helps the industry as a whole to grow and communicate. It is also critical for suppliers of those particular industries to understand the standards to which they are being held.

ISO 9000

A good QM system is based on eight principles that are outlined in *The International Organization for Standardization (ISO)* document, entitled *ISO 9000*. ISO is a network of the national standards institutes of 148 countries, represented by one member per country, with a central secretariat in Geneva, Switzerland, that coordinates the system. The ISO 9000 family of standards was developed to assist organizations of all types and sizes to implement and operate effective QM systems. The eight QM principles listed in the ISO 9000 document are:

- Customer focus
- Leadership
- Involvement of people
- Process approach
- System approach to management
- Continuous improvement
- Factual approach to decision making
- Mutually beneficial supplier relationships

Because customer needs and expectations are always changing and because of competition and technical advances, businesses must constantly improve their products and processes. According to ISO, the QM system used should encourage businesses to explore customer requirements, define the processes that help produce a product or service that is acceptable to the customer, and keep these processes running as planned. A good QM system can provide the framework for continual improvement to increase customer satisfaction. It can demonstrate to the business and its customers that this company is able to provide products or services that consistently meet their needs. To do this, ISO 9000 provides a framework that allows organizations to develop a documented, controlled, understood, standardized approach to managing quality, rather than the commonly seen freewheeling, unstructured approach—an approach often utilized by middle managers who have gained their positions based on outstanding individual contributions but who lack management experience or formal training.

Process documentation is core to ISO 9000. A process is any activity, or set of activities, that uses resources to transform inputs into outputs. An example of a simple process is making a peanut butter and jelly sandwich. The inputs are bread, jelly, and peanut butter. The resource needed is a knife. The activities are spreading the jelly and peanut butter onto the bread and putting the bread together to create a sandwich. This is an oversimplified example. Sometimes processes are extremely complicated and sensitive such that if one process step is completed incorrectly or if it is skipped, the resulting output will not meet the intended customer need.

In business, often the output of one process becomes the input of the next related process. For instance, the making of the peanut butter and jelly sandwich described above is only one part of the entire meal. Perhaps you also need to make iced tea, a fruit salad, and chocolate cake. Perhaps you had to make homemade peanut butter using peanuts. You might also need to set the table and invite a friend. Each of these tasks represents a process, and all of the interrelated processes must be completed accurately to ensure that the entire process of "having a friend over for lunch" is achieved. A business adopts a Process Approach when it systematically identifies and manages its processes and pays particular attention to the interactions among those processes.

Baldrige Criteria

The United States Congress established the Criteria for Performance Excellence in 1987 as part of the Malcolm Baldrige National Quality Award program. The program was created to recognize U.S. organizations for their achievements in quality and performance and to raise awareness about the importance of quality and performance excellence as a competitive edge.

For 15 years, the Baldrige Criteria have been used by thousands of U.S. organizations to stay abreast of ever-increasing competition and to improve performance. For today's business environment, the criteria have been updated to help organizations respond to current challenges: openness and transparency in governance and ethics; the need to create value for customers and the business; and the challenges of rapid innovation and capitalizing on knowledge assets. Whether a business is small or large, is involved in service or manufacturing, or has one office or multiple sites across the globe, the criteria provide a valuable framework that can help plan in an uncertain environment.

The criteria are designed to help organizations use an integrated approach to organizational performance management that results in:

- Delivery of ever-improving value to customers, contributing to market-place success
- Improvement of overall organizational effectiveness and capabilities
- Organizational and personal learning

The core values and concepts of the Baldrige Criteria are embodied in the seven categories below:

1. Leadership
2. Strategic planning
3. Customer and market focus
4. Measurement, analysis, and knowledge management
5. Human resources focus
6. Process management
7. Business results

To determine how well they meet the Baldrige Criteria, many organizations perform a self-assessment. The self-assessment scoring system places 450 points out of 1,000 total points on business results. This demonstrates a fundamental emphasis on results when assessing performance of an organization. All other positives must ultimately contribute to the business results of the organization. A common stock comparison study has shown a correlation between the use of Baldrige Criteria and improved stock market performance, which demonstrates that Baldrige Criteria–based organizations are high performers. A comparison of Baldrige Award recipients to the Standard & Poor's 500 (S&P 500) shows that the 24 publicly traded 1988–1998 Baldrige Award recipients, as a group, outperformed the S&P 500 by approximately 3.8 to 1. The six publicly traded whole company award recipients, as a group, outperformed the S&P 500 by approximately 4.8 to 1. The 70 publicly traded 1990–1998 site-visited applicants, as a group, outperformed the S&P 500 by approximately 2 to 1. The group of 14 publicly traded whole company site-visited applicants outperformed the S&P 500 by almost 2.2 to 1.

Following is an abbreviated list of outstanding organizations that have received the award:

- Motorola, Inc.
- Boeing Airlift and Tanker Programs
- 3M Dental Products Division
- Merrill Lynch Credit Corporation
- Xerox Business Services

- AT&T Consumer Communications Services
- Eastman Chemical Company
- Ritz-Carlton Hotel Company
- Federal Express Corporation
- Texas Instruments, Inc.

Quality Systems Support Six Sigma Efforts

So what do ISO 9000 and the Baldrige Criteria have to do with Six Sigma? Along with Six Sigma, ISO 9000 and the Baldrige Criteria are the most highly implemented quality management systems and philosophies in industry. While they are each unique, it is interesting how closely the underlying concepts of all three center around the following:

1. Process focus
2. Customer focus
3. Collaboration
4. Data driven management
5. Strategic planning for quality

Table 1.1 incorporates the key concepts of ISO 9000, the Baldrige Criteria, and Six Sigma into these five critical concepts.

Table 1.1   Comparison of Key Concepts

Common Concepts	ISO 9000	Malcolm Baldrige Criteria for Performance Excellence	Essential Themes of Six Sigma
Process focus	Customer focus Process approach Continual improvement	Leadership Process management	Process focus, management and improvement
Customer focus	Mutually beneficial supplier relationships	Customer and market focus	Genuine focus on the customer
Collaboration	Involvement of people	Human resources focus	Boundaryless collaboration
Data driven management	Factual approach to decision making	Measurement, analysis, and knowledge management	Data- and fact-driven management
Strategic planning for quality	Leadership System approach to management	Strategic planning Business results	Proactive management Drive for perfection Tolerance for failure

Table 1.2 provides a more focused look at the similarities of the Baldrige Criteria and Six Sigma.

Table 1.2 Similarities between Six Sigma and the Baldrige Criteria

Six Sigma	Baldrige Criteria	Similarities
Genuine focus on the customer	Customer and market focus	Six Sigma and Baldrige are very similar in this regard. Both place utmost importance on customer focus. They both focus on accurate identification of internal and external customers and the importance of understanding the customer's need and desires. Both call for customer-focused results. Six Sigma improvements are defined by their impact on customer satisfaction. Baldrige expects customer-focused results and looks for indicators of customer-perceived value.
Data- and fact-driven management	Measurement, analysis, and knowledge management	Both focus on the use of metrics to drive business decisions. The metrics are determined based on customer needs and expectations. Both are based on the concept of "management by fact."
Process focus, management and improvement	Process management	Both strongly support an understanding of processes and management of processes (by facts).
Proactive management	Strategic planning	Both systems strongly support strategic, proactive management planning. They both communicate that organizations should be proactively addressing customer expectations, expected changes, etc. Furthermore, both support these activities through managing by facts.
Boundaryless collaboration	Human resources	Both systems promote collaboration. The Work Systems subcategory of Baldrige focuses on how the organization's work and jobs enable employees and the organization to achieve high performance through cooperation, empowerment, and innovation. This and the other human resource aspects work together to promote a culture of collaboration. Baldrige also promotes this in its focus on process management.
Drive for perfection Tolerance for failure	Strategic planning	The two systems are similar in this area with regard to driving for perfection. The DMAIC cycle provides a methodology or strategy to improve processes. Baldrige expects business results and strategic planning.

Because of the underlying similarities among the key quality management philosophies that have dominated in the manufacturing industry, some believe Six Sigma is merely a set of recycled statistical and project management tools that includes team charters, Voice of the Customer methods, diagrams, Pareto charts, histograms, control charts, and flowcharts. They believe that Six Sigma has simply made traditional statistical tools available to the industry masses. Yet others believe that Six Sigma is a quality management system that can transform organizational culture and the bottom line through accurate identification of customer needs and managing core business processes by data to ensure those needs are met. Actually, Six Sigma is all of the above.

Six Sigma got its name from a statistical concept, but the approach goes well beyond data and figures. With that said, we can't move forward without understanding just what *six sigma* is and what it says about processes.

In statistics, the lowercase Greek letter sigma "σ" is the symbol for standard deviation, which describes the degree of variation in a data set, a group of items, or a process. A six sigma level of quality means that there are fewer than 3.4 defects, or deviations from the standard, per million units produced. It is a technical measure of customer satisfaction.

A unit can be any product or service, or your job's deliverables. The principles of Six Sigma can be applied to many different situations. Consider geltabs as an example. If, in a sample of 100 geltabs, five defects were found, that would mean 0.05 or 5 percent defects, or that 95 percent of units were acceptable. According to the sigma conversion table (see Table 1.3), this percentage of acceptable units falls between sigma levels 3 and 4. At a three sigma level, you can expect 66,807 defects per 1 million geltabs, and at a four sigma level you can expect 6,210 defects per 1 million geltabs.

The management philosophy that has grown up around the six sigma measurement described above focuses on customer satisfaction, data driven management, and process improvement. Customer satisfaction is the key determinant of

Table 1.3   Six Sigma Conversions

Percentage of Acceptable Units	Sigma Level	Defects/Million Units
99.99966	6σ	3.4
99.98	5σ	233
99.4	4σ	6,210
93.3	3σ	66,807
69.1	2σ	308,537
30.9	1σ	690,000

quality. If a product satisfies the customer or meets the customer's specifications, then it is acceptable. Otherwise, it is defective in some way. To define the quality of any product, one must fully understand customer needs and specifications. Accurate identification of customer requirements is the heart of Six Sigma philosophy. In order to calculate a sigma level that realistically reflects customer satisfaction, you must understand what your customer wants. For example, a unit that is perfect in your eyes may not be perfect in the eyes of your customer.

So Six Sigma *does* provide the tools—some new, some old—but it also prescribes a step-by-step methodology for their application. Using the DMAIC cycle, Six Sigma ties those tools together into a neat package that can be applied across many functions and industries. If applied correctly with the key focus on processes and customers, it can also work at different organizational levels where scope is clearly defined. Applying a strategy that centers on the use of collaboration and data driven management can bring Six Sigma into the world of middle management.

The Bottom Line

- Do not accept the notion that the underlying concepts of Six Sigma cannot be implemented without high-level support. Middle managers can create a Six Sigma organization in their own backyard.
- In order to fully appreciate the underlying concepts of Six Sigma, an understanding of basic quality management principles is needed.
- A quality management (QM) system is a tool used by management designed to ensure product quality and customer satisfaction.
- A system is the organizational structure, responsibilities, procedures, and resources needed to conduct a major function within a business or to support a common business need.
- Systems are usually made up of many major processes that take an input, add value to it, and produce an output.
- Along with Six Sigma, ISO 9000 and the Baldrige Criteria are the most highly implemented quality management systems and philosophies in industry. While they are each unique, it is interesting how closely the underlying concepts of all three center around the following:
  - Process focus
  - Customer focus
  - Collaboration
  - Data driven management
  - Strategic planning for quality

Chapter 2

Six Sigma Tools and Deliverables for the Self-Empowered Manager

Never confuse motion with action.

—Ernest Hemingway

As functional managers, we've been taught to deliver, to make things happen. In fact, early delivery and early accomplishment are praised. Of course, we want quality. But at some point, the business culture we swim through daily turns into a crowd of faceless executives reviewing our deliverables and reading our résumés to determine if we have delivered enough to warrant moving to the next level. We all know how it is, ultimately. This mindset keeps us moving, but are we moving forward? There exists a constant struggle between completing the tasks at hand and creating the time to develop and test new ideas and processes. The development time that slows us down but promises delayed gratification keeps us fearful that senior management will not understand delays. It's in this mindset—this dilemma—that we find ourselves interested in the concepts of Six Sigma and the mandate that we must first obtain senior management's approval and support. Some of us are functioning in this state when we are paid a visit by an assigned Six Sigma Black Belt or quality consultant. Because we're in a hurry to produce, he or she seems to drag out every point with new buzzwords and phrases, extra steps, and exercises. Black Belts and quality management consultants thrive on the up-front work that promises our long-term success. Innately we wonder if all can be accomplished in some sort of condensed, more down-to-earth fashion.

Well, it can. We just have to know how to do it. Accomplishing our quality goals should be straightforward, efficient, and productive. We don't always have an extra hour to spare hashing out the goal statement versus the opportunity statement for a project that's already on the books. We may already know what the goal is and why it must be done—we just need to communicate it effectively to our organization. We need to map out a plan and get started. The Six Sigma tool kit provides many useful tools and deliverables that can help us accomplish our goals. Just as Six Sigma methodology asks that we cut process steps that are nonproductive, we can also condense and alter the tools to fit our own organizational needs.

Six Sigma prescribes the use of specific project management and statistical tools for each stage of the DMAIC (define, measure, analyze, improve, and control) cycle. These tools make up the Six Sigma tool kit. Many of the tools have been around for quite some time. According to Six Sigma philosophy, numerous tools are provided so that the Black Belt and team can select the ones that are value-added and make the most sense given the project at hand. Armed with a general understanding of these tools, the functional manager is often the best judge for determining which ones are value-added for a given situation. Managers have the best handle on the issues facing our own organizations, the priorities, and current workload. If the general rule is to "keep it simple," the best tools for everyday use by managers should be easy to understand, use, and explain to the staff.

The DMAIC cycle is a useful approach for self-empowered managers because it lays the foundation for a Six Sigma-based program that can be applied to any scope of work. Traditional Six Sigma prescribes the use of particular statistical and project management tools for each stage of the DMAIC cycle. A subset of the tools is listed in Table 2.1.

Just as traditional Six Sigma can be applied across industries in manufacturing and nonmanufacturing (or service) arenas, the self-empowered manager can apply Six Sigma to his or her personal situation. When applying Six Sigma DMAIC tools to your own organization, you will need to decide which tools are most useful given your job scope and responsibilities. Some of the tools are easier to use than others. Managers who have a strong background in statistics will naturally feel more comfortable applying more complex statistical methods. However, one does not need to be a statistical whiz to make use of the basic tools. Following are some of the key Six Sigma tools that do not require in-depth understanding of statistics to implement. These tools also support the manager's goal to infuse the five basic quality concepts (process focus, customer focus, collaboration, data driven management, and strategic thinking) into his or her organization. It is up to the manager to determine how formal the activities should be. This will depend on the organization culture, size, and level of responsibility.

Table 2.1 Common Traditional Six Sigma DMAIC Tools

DMAIC Stage	Six Sigma Tools
Define	Brainstorming Project Charter Project Plan Gantt chart Affinity diagramming Voice of the Customer methods (VOC) Project stakeholder analysis High-level process map (SIPOC diagram)
Measure	Sampling Detailed process map or flowchart Data forms and spreadsheets Operational Definitions Sigma calculation worksheet Measurement systems analysis (MSA)
Analyze	Brainstorming Process flow analysis Value- and non-value-added analysis Detailed process maps or flowcharts Pareto analysis and chart Histogram or frequency plot Scatter plot or correlation diagram Run chart, Trend chart, Time plot Cause-and-effect analysis (fishbone) Relations diagram Stratified charts Process manipulation/experimental worksheet Process value and time analysis Regression and correlation analysis Multivariate study Analysis of variance (ANOVA) Chi-squared test Cost-benefit analysis Gage R & R (repeatability and reproducibility)
Improve	Implementation planning Failure mode effect analysis (FMEA) Stakeholder analysis Process documentation Advanced creative techniques Impact/Effort Matrix Force field analysis Pilot testing debrief Design of experiments (DOE)
Control	Process documentation checklists Control Charts Process management chart Response plan worksheet Metric Scorecards or Dashboards

Define Stage

Project Charter—Key Concepts: Process Focus and Strategic Planning

Six Sigma projects begin with a Project Charter. The charter generally includes the business case, a problem or opportunity statement, a goal statement, and the project scope. The charter can also identify the team leader, team members, key stakeholders, and milestones. Identification of these key elements early on is critical to project success. It allows the team to clarify and formalize their agreement and mutual understanding of the project. If your personal organization is large enough to warrant formation of teams, a Project Charter is an easy, quick tool that is value-added. To reduce the time spent on this activity, the charter can be limited to goals, scope, and business case, as appropriate.

Project Plan—Key Concepts: Process Focus and Strategic Planning

If your personal organization is small, each person can develop a simplified charter document or Project Plan that includes key details for completion of individual projects. At a minimum, the Project Plan should include the project goal, business case, and milestones. This will allow you and your employees to gain a common understanding and agreement of their individual projects.

Voice of the Customer (VOC) Methods— Key Concept: Customer Focus

What "Voice of the Customer Analysis" boils down to for the functional manager is asking your customers what they want and need from your personal organization. Many times, managers believe they already know the answers to these critical questions. This may be because the manager's responsibilities have been passed down through organization changes, a promotion, or by joining the company at the management level. There is often a learning curve associated with new responsibilities or an increase in scope. In general, it takes six months to a year for a new manager to become established in an organization depending on the level of experience and how closely related his or her past experiences are to the new responsibilities. The opposite scenario also exists. There are managers who have been around for years, diligently managing the same processes. They don't see a compelling reason to question the process or their customers. In this case, having the "If it ain't broke, don't fix it" mentality may be preventing process improvement. Finding out what your customers want and need may be as simple as scheduling a meeting and asking them directly. When possible, the best option is to sit face to face with your customers. For organizations that have many customers, group meetings to obtain feedback and surveys are useful options.

Brainstorming—Key Concept: Collaboration

The purpose of brainstorming is to create a list of new ideas or options for a task or solution. Although a serious exercise, all participants should be encouraged to "toss out" ideas, think beyond the here and now, and not worry about the perceptions of others. Creativity should be the primary goal. Often someone will share an idea that isn't quite right, but a coworker may add to it or alter it. Together they create a perfect initial thought and come up with a unique plan, solution, or idea that works. This technique encourages collaboration within the organization and helps build a culture of creativity.

Affinity Diagramming—Key Concept: Collaboration

Affinity diagramming is the process of grouping similar items. Similar to brain-storming, this tool encourages creative thinking. Each participant can quietly write down thoughts, ideas, options, and so forth on sticky notes. Then, either as individuals or as a team, they can group like items together. This is a helpful way to organize thoughts so that logical next steps can be determined.

High-Level Process Map (SIPOC Diagram)— Key Concepts: Process and Customer Focus

A SIPOC (suppliers, inputs, process, outputs, and customers) diagram is a quick and easy way to help identify the suppliers, inputs, outputs, and customers for each of your key processes. A SIPOC can be helpful in identifying the boundaries of a process and the critical elements without getting into too much detail. It helps keep the focus on the big picture when trying to identify the organization's key deliverables and customers.

Measure Stage

Sampling—Key Concepts: Data Driven Management and Strategy Planning

Sampling allows for measurement of a relatively few units compared to measuring every unit. Testing, reviewing, or counting each and every unit in a process can be extremely time consuming and illogical for any organization. There are many sampling strategies that can be applied, depending on the unique situation. But a general sampling method that works in most functional level scenarios is to define a unit, determine the average number of units for a particular time frame, and then refer to a standard sampling table to determine how many units should be tested, reviewed, or counted to obtain the desired level of confidence that the quality of your sample will reflect the entire population.

Data Collection Forms and Spreadsheets— Key Concept: Data Driven Management

Data Collection Forms are used to collect and organize data. They can also serve as checklists to ensure that all details of the unit (whatever you are focusing on) are reviewed, measured, counted, etc. Data Collection Forms should capture the appropriate data and be easy to use. Spreadsheets can be created and used to compile data collected on the individual Data Collection Forms. The easiest software that is routinely available now is Microsoft Excel, although there are other, more sophisticated software packages available. When possible, keep forms to a minimum.

Operational Definitions—Key Concepts: Collaboration, Data Driven Management, and Strategic Planning

To ensure that all parties understand the measurements or metrics you have selected to track and analyze, it is important to have a clear, detailed, and understandable description of what the data means. A clear description will also ensure that data is gathered consistently. This is critical for data analysis and communication of metrics.

Analysis Stage

Value- and Non-Value-Added Analysis—Key Concepts: Customer Focus and Strategic Planning

When evaluating a process or making a process decision, the manager should always consider whether a step or action is value-added for the customer. In a regulatory environment, this should also be a regulatory risk versus value discussion. If a large chunk of organizational time is spent on an activity that adds little value and is a low regulatory risk, perhaps time is better spent elsewhere.

Detailed Process Maps or Flowcharts— Key Concept: Process Focus

It is critical to understand the detailed "as-is" process. Starting with the high-level steps in your SIPOC diagram, you can work with your staff to create highly detailed process maps. A handy way to do this as a team is to brainstorm to think of all the detailed process steps, write them on sticky notes, and then stick them on the wall in "as-is" order. Once the "as-is" flowchart is created, gaps can be explored and addressed to create a "should-be" process. If possible, it is best to create flowcharts using software; however paper and pencil is a good place to start. Now you're ready for Process Flow Analysis.

Process Flow Analysis—Key Concepts: Process Focus and Collaboration

Once you've created an "as-is" process flowchart, you and your staff can begin to evaluate the process looking for redundancies, and unnecessary hand-offs, steps, or decisions. You can also evaluate steps that may be creating backlogs, rework delays, and so on. At the functional level, this discussion can be held at staff meetings or one-on-one meetings with the responsible people. Depending on the size and scope of your personal organization, all processes may not be documented. At a minimum, sketching the process flow with pen and paper is an extremely useful visual to aid discussions about even minor processes.

Pareto Analysis and Chart—Key Concept: Data Driven Management

A Pareto chart is an easy way to show the relative importance of causes, defects, and other aspects of a process. The chart is based on the rule of thumb coined by Italian economist, Vilfredo Pareto. He said that 80 percent of all problems result from 20 percent of the causes (commonly known as the 80/20 rule). For example, if errors are categorized into types or causes, a Pareto chart is merely a visual method to show the breakdown of causes for error and the frequency of each, as shown in Figure 2.1.

On a small scale, you may not need to graph this data to see which 20 percent are causing 80 percent of the issues or problems. However, it is extremely useful for presentation purposes. Remember to keep it simple; don't graph anything you don't need to graph.

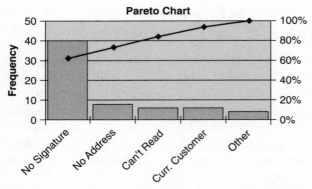

Figure 2.1 Pareto charts assist with identifying categories of issues or problems that, if solved, will provide the greatest benefit based on Vilfredo Pareto's 80/20 rule.

Improve Stage

Impact/Effort Matrix—Key Concepts: Strategic Planning and Collaboration

Creating an Impact/Effort Matrix is helpful when facing competing actions or solutions. Armed with a list of solutions, you and your staff can discuss each in terms of impact and effort. The impact and effort levels involved can be rated on a scale of one to four. The group should discuss questions such as:

- For Impact—
  - Will our customer notice this benefit? Immediately? In the long term?
  - Will choosing this option bring noticeable relief to those working downstream in the process?
  - Does the solution impact the biggest issues for the process?
- For Effort—
  - Is this solution or change easy to implement?
  - What are the resource implications?
  - Do we have the technology in place to implement this solution?

Once ratings are given to each solution or option, they can be evaluated using Figure 2.2 to determine which options are most feasible, given their impact and the effort required. Write each solution or option in the appropriate quadrant based on the ratings it was given. Look to quadrant two to find the solutions or options that will require the least amount of effort for the greatest impact.

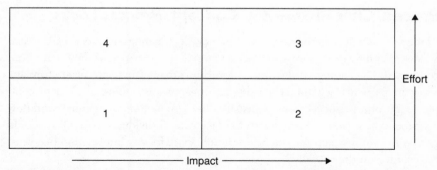

Figure 2.2 An Impact/Effort Matrix can be used to determine which solutions or ideas require the least effort and provide the greatest impact.

Solutions or options landing in quadrant four should be avoided since they will have the least impact but require the greatest amount of effort.

Pilot Testing — Key Concepts: Strategic Planning and Process Focus

When possible, any process change should be piloted prior to full implementation. This is critical to ensure that all bases have been covered and the process will work as envisioned. Piloting a process on a smaller scale allows for details to be ironed out, technological solutions to be tested, and the overall process to be validated. For more minor processes or for smaller scope projects, pilots can often be conducted informally and quickly.

Control Stage

Process Documentation — Key Concept: Process Focus

Once you have determined the "should-be" process flow, it is important to document the process in a Standard Operating Practice (SOP) or a Standard Working Practice (SWP) (also sometimes called "Job Aids"). Explaining the process in more detail or in a more narrative form is critical to ensure ongoing process consistency. It is extremely useful for training new staff and for providing long-standing staff a guide to refer to periodically or use day to day, depending on the complexity of your processes. Most highly regulated industries are required to have SOPs; however, even if a regulatory agency doesn't require them, they are valuable tools for any organization.

Process Checklists—Key Concept: Process Focus

Along with developing flowcharts and process documentation, Process Checklists are essential for many processes. Process Checklists ensure that all steps have been completed. Depending on the process, checklists may or may not be appropriate. They are particularly helpful for redundant processes including many steps completed by one person. Process Checklists are also useful for manual workflow processes where paperwork is handed off to many individuals. Checklists should be easy to complete and should include ample space for any information that must be recorded on the checklist.

Control Charts—Key Concept: Data Driven Management

The Control Chart is the fundamental tool of statistical process control. It indicates the normal range of variability that is expected in a process. Thus it aids the organization in determining if a process is operating consistently. Expected variability is also called "common cause" variability. A Control Chart has acceptable limits of variability referred to as lower control limit (LCL) and upper control limit (UCL). As shown in Figure 2.3, data points that fall outside the LCL and UCL indicate

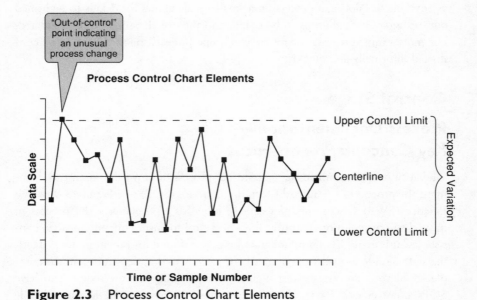

Figure 2.3   Process Control Chart Elements

unusual or "special cause" variability that should be investigated. These causes can then be identified and eliminated to bring the process back under control.

A process is considered to be in control if all variation is random and if it conforms to the three basic rules below:

- No data points are outside the control limits.
- No runs of seven data points ascending or descending. This is evidence that a change is occurring in the process.
- No trends of seven data points above or below the mean. This is evidence that a process has shifted.

Metric Dashboards — Key Concept: Data Driven Management

Any organization, regardless of scope, can create metrics for their key deliverables. A Metric Dashboard is merely a template for communicating those metrics to the applicable audiences. The scope of your responsibility will dictate how sophisticated your Metric Dashboards should be. A Dashboard is usually a one-page table that lists the metrics being tracked, the metric data for each time frame, and the target metric. Metrics that are at risk or unacceptable can be highlighted.

As the Champion of your personal organization, you are responsible for understanding your processes. You are expected to proactively identify and evaluate issues, whether they are daily issues that are easily resolved or those long-standing issues that beg for resolution but often get pushed to the back burner because of ongoing priorities. There are also hidden issues lurking within the workflow that negatively impact productivity and efficiency. In many cases, identification and resolution of these hidden issues can have a positive impact on the two preceding categories. For this reason, it's important for managers to pay attention to and understand the processes within their scope of work.

Traditionally, Six Sigma projects begin with a Project Charter. However, to apply Six Sigma concepts within your own scope of work, it may be more helpful to begin with identification of your core processes and customers. It doesn't really matter what format you use, the most critical thing is to understand the SIPOC concept. Remember to keep it simple! If you manage a very small group, you can sit down and discuss the SIPOC criteria for your key processes. The advantage of writing it down is creating a common visual to document the discussion. Within a SIPOC diagram, your process steps should be limited to the key five to seven high-level steps. The visual SIPOC is also useful for presentation purposes. If your personal organization is large enough to warrant teams, you can require a visual SIPOC from the team; this will demonstrate that they have completed the SIPOC discussion for their assigned process. Once you choose a template for your SIPOCs, one can easily be created for each key process for which you and your personal organization are responsible.

Regardless of the format chosen, the following list provides the key steps for developing a SIPOC:

1. Name the process to be mapped out.
2. Define the scope of the process.
3. Name the suppliers and the inputs they provide.
4. Establish five to seven "high-level" process steps to describe the process.
5. Name the outputs and the customers that receive them.

There are numerous examples of SIPOC formats in the published literature. Some of the best available are:

- *The Six Sigma Way* by Peter Pande, Robert Neuman, and Roland Cavanagh
- *The Six Sigma Way Team Fieldbook* by Peter Pande, Robert Neuman, and Roland Cavanaugh
- *Six Sigma for Everyone* by George Eckes

These books also include excellent templates and formats for other Six Sigma tools.

Using the DMAIC model for managers described in Chapter 1, Table 2.2 breaks down each stage into Six Sigma deliverables that are particularly useful to managers.

Each of the deliverables listed above can be developed using key tools found in the Six Sigma tool kit.

The Bottom Line

- Six Sigma prescribes the use of specific project management and statistical tools for each stage of the DMAIC cycle. These tools make up the Six Sigma tool kit.
- The Six Sigma tool kit provides many useful deliverables and/or tools that can help us accomplish our goals. Just as Six Sigma methodology asks that we cut process steps that are nonproductive, we can also condense and alter the tools to fit our own organizational needs.
- Use of Six Sigma tools should be easy, efficient, and productive.
- The DMAIC cycle is a useful approach for self-empowered managers because it lays the foundation for a Six Sigma-based program that can be applied to any scope of work.

Table 2.2 Key Six Sigma Deliverables for Middle Managers

DMAIC Stage	Self-Empowered Managers	Recommended Deliverables
Define	As the Manager/Champion, you can identify, evaluate, and select "Problem or Improvement Projects" for your staff and work with them to ensure that they understand the issues and your mission. These problems or opportunities for improvement can be documented in a project plan. For a larger staff (i.e., 20 or more), team charters can be developed. You are the Champion of your personal organization.	• Voice of Customer Analysis • DMAIC Project Plan or Charter with problem statement and scope • Initial SIPOC diagram with high-level process, defined scope, suppliers, and customers.
Measure	You can work with your staff to map out the process and collect baseline performance data. Then you can determine what metrics should be measured and how the data will be collected. Remember to keep it simple!	• Final SIPOC for process with inputs and outputs identified • Data Collection Plan 　• Identification of metrics 　• Identification and operational definition of metrics 　• Data Collection Forms 　• Data spreadsheets
Analyze	You or a designee can analyze the "as-is" process determining where there may be gaps, unnecessary hand-offs, etc. In discussing how to improve the process, you can evaluate value-added versus non-value-added steps and options for process improvement.	• "As-is" process map (flowchart) • Process Flow Analysis • Value-Added vs. Non-Value-Added *(including risk)* Analysis
Improve	Once you have determined the best process based on the data you have tracked, you can diagram and pilot the new process.	• Improved process map (flowchart) • Pilot run information/ learning
Control	You can document and implement the process. Then you can continue to track appropriate metrics to determine whether the new process is holding up over time. If your data demonstrates a "dip" in performance, you can investigate and take appropriate action.	• Standard Operating Procedure • Control data collection plan 　• Metric targets 　• Data Collection Forms 　• Data spreadsheets 　• Metrics Report Template 　• Metrics scorecard

- It's up to the manager to determine how formal the activities required for use of the tools should be. This will depend on the organization culture, size, and level of responsibility.
- Traditionally, Six Sigma projects begin with a Project Charter. However, to apply Six Sigma concepts within your own scope of work, it's more helpful to begin with identification of your core processes and customers.

Chapter 3

Advantages of Adopting Six Sigma Concepts

Even if you're on the right track, you'll get run over if you just sit there.
—Will Rogers, Humorist

Many leading companies such as J&J, Home Depot, 3M, and Quest Diagnostics are setting the standard for Six Sigma implementation by driving initiatives from the top down. In following this objective, the commonly provided benefits of implementing Six Sigma are skewed toward those that will interest top management. We most often hear the following five advantages of Six Sigma:

1. Generates sustained success demonstrated by double-digit growth and strong market share
2. Sets a common performance goal for the entire organization—near perfect quality
3. Executes strategic change demonstrated by new products, launching new ventures, entering new markets, etc.
4. Increases revenue by satisfying customers
5. Focuses on improving quality by reducing errors, thus inspiring employees, instilling a particular culture and attitude into the company, creating an image in the market and community, and attracting investors

Middle managers should, of course, care about these advantages, but down in the trenches, where the day-to-day processes are taking place, these important but somewhat removed goals don't tend to be the focus. Managers generally know that these items contribute to the bottom line in our companies, but we're so busy just trying to produce the products and services that we're forced to focus on the day-to-day issues. After all, isn't that the job? Isn't that what managers are hired to do? However, most managers share another overwhelming focus that keeps us going: the belief and hope that we'll rise to the next level of management if we continue to do a great job. Once we arrive, we'll worry about the market share, revenue, and double-digit growth.

"So what is in it for me?" you might ask. This is not a selfish question; it's a strategic one. It's a question that complements the idea of bringing quality management to a more personal level. Paradigms will begin to shift the day you wake up convinced that your work will be made easier by focusing attention on the concepts of process focus, customer focus, collaboration, data driven management, and strategic planning. You'll begin to see that quality is what you do as a manager; it's your job and not someone else's. The phrase *quality management* will become obsolete. Managing quality will become another spoke in the wheel of plain old management.

Most of us have heard the phenomenal results of traditional Six Sigma methodology. The increase to the bottom line, so appealing to top management, inspired us to pay attention. While the exciting results typically shared are critical for catching the eyes of top executives, they support the notion that we must have top management involvement and support to implement Six Sigma. The examples provided draw us back to the top layer of the company and make us question our ability to personally make a difference. Consider these impressive examples from one of the best selling Six Sigma books of all time, *The Six Sigma Way:*

- From the initial year or so of break-even efforts, the payoff for GE has accelerated: $750 million by the end of 1998, a forecasted $1.5 billion by the end of 1999, and expectations of more billions down the road.
- At Motorola, in the decade between Six Sigma's beginning in 1987 and 1997, achievements included a five-fold growth in sales, with profits climbing nearly 20 percent, cumulative savings based on Six Sigma efforts pegged at $14 billion, and Motorola stock price gains compounded to an annual rate of 21.3 percent.
- By 1999, AlliedSignal was saving more than $600 million a year, thanks to the widespread employee training in and application of Six Sigma principles

So what are middle managers to do once they've heard these impressive examples and decided that the concepts are worth exploring? Your choices are (1) to gain top management support for rolling out Six Sigma methodologies across the company, requiring a huge initial investment and temporary stress to the organization or (2) to implement the concepts within your own organization. To have the dedication and focus needed to infuse the key concepts underlying Six Sigma into your own organization, you should fully understand how doing so will benefit you on several levels. To be the leader or Champion of a personal initiative to adopt a new management philosophy based on Six Sigma concepts, you must have a strong internal drive toward the direction in which you want to lead others.

Those of us who've been in management for a while have heard the question, "If it ain't broke, why fix it?" quite a few times. We usually hear it as an example of how we *shouldn't* think. But why *should* we spend our valuable time fixing things that aren't broken? The answer most often presented is that we should strive for continuous improvement; we should always try to improve what we're doing, how we're doing it, and our deliverables. This can be said of our processes, our management style, our methods of communication, anything. At the functional level, this philosophy can certainly be applied. But frankly, some processes may have reached near perfection because they are particularly straightforward, have a unique customer, or require minimal inputs or steps. For those types of processes, rather than "If it ain't broke, why fix it?" perhaps the question should be "Does this process still meet the need?" When you begin to question, interview, and survey your internal and external customers, you may learn that your near perfect process is like an outfit that was hip 20 years ago, but in today's environment it's lackluster at best. (Sometimes the one wearing the outfit is the last to know.) In fact, you may have inherited that outfit in a culture where it still seems cool. But if you step out into a bigger world of possibilities, you'll find that you're in dire need of a makeover. In fact, your broader organization may also need a makeover. So whether you suspect that your processes, management style, or methods of communication can be improved, or you suspect that it's all pretty good, taking a close look is an excellent idea on multiple levels.

Infusing the five basic concepts underlying Six Sigma and the associated methodologies and tools into your own organization will help you reach your professional goals. Of course, one should be loyal to the broader organization and hope to contribute to its overall success, but in today's environment the majority of workers no longer stay at the same company for 20 or 30 years. Companies seem to merge more often than ever before. Depending on your field, you may be forced to change companies to develop and move forward in your career. By streamlining your processes by implementing a Six Sigma-based process focus, you may be able to take on additional responsibilities by utilizing staff more efficiently. There will be less fire fighting on a daily basis because you will have identified and addressed root causes. You can empower your Process Leads to take responsibility for their assigned processes, freeing you up to take on higher-level responsibilities. Your internal customers will support you because you care about what they want. It will be easier to gain customer buy-in, when necessary, because you have taken the time to build strong relationships following customer-focused and collaborative Six Sigma concepts. If your customers believe that you care about their needs, they will be more open to discussing your viewpoints when compromise is necessary. This will lead to more win-win situations. People will enjoy working for you because you value their input. Difficult people will be exposed via a natural process; they will begin to stand out in your organization. Your accomplishments will be supported by facts and data. You will have proof that you can get the job done while making improvements. Facts will show that you can make things happen! Your résumé will become more impressive. Over time your supervisor will see that you are a strategic thinker, can plan and execute projects, and lead others to do so.

By implementing processes at the functional level that allow for data driven management, you will create valuable business metrics to support the accomplishments of your team. Accomplishments backed by data will not only impress your current supervisor but will also impress those considering you for higher levels of responsibility. Business metrics provide proof that you can handle responsibility, impact the organization, and get the job at hand accomplished. Data allows your personal organization to stand out in the crowd; it proves that you know how to get results! Many people in low to middle management positions include responsibilities such as the following on their résumés:

- Served as Drug Safety representative on the global implementation team
- Managed staff of 10
- Reviewed and approved regulatory reports
- Compiled monthly batch reports

By implementing the key concepts of Six Sigma into your day-to-day work, your résumé can begin to move from entries such as those listed above to statements that show what you *have accomplished* not simply what you are responsible for. Examples of this are:

- As subteam lead on the global implementation team, authored Primer for Drug Safety Compliance
- Led staff of 10 in streamlining three key processes
- Improved quality of regulatory reports
- Led team to compile all batch reports on time

Accomplishments are vague if not supported by data. There is power in numbers! For example, how do you know that you streamlined your process? How do you know that you improved the quality of regulatory reports? As you move forward in your career and wish to take on added responsibilities, implement additional changes, or gain a higher position in a new company, you will need to instill confidence in the decision makers. Here is the list of accomplishments taken one step further:

- As subteam lead on the global implementation team, authored Primer for Drug Safety Compliance that was distributed to 100,000 employees worldwide
- Led staff of 10 in efforts to streamline key process by reducing handoffs by 25 percent and increasing cycle time by 50 percent
- Improved quality of regulatory reports by reducing errors from an average of 10 errors per page to 2 errors per page
- Led team to compile 100 percent of lot reports on time, representing a 50 percent improvement over a six-month period

As your scope of responsibility increases, you will, most likely, be expected to manage more individuals, whether directly or indirectly. Your personal organization will grow and with that growth comes great opportunity to show your leadership potential. Leadership is a critical component to the success of top managers (e.g., vice presidents, presidents, CEOs). Beyond their ability to make excellent decisions, forecast and create strategic plans, and communicate effectively lies their ability to inspire others to perform, to *want* to perform, and to want to perform *for them*. In addition, at higher levels, interpersonal skills are critical because successful cross-functional, cross-affiliate, and cross-regional interactions are necessary on a day-to-day basis. These leaders had to start somewhere. It may have been in your office. Remember how in high school they told us that students with B averages and excellent interpersonal skills will become more successful than straight A students with poor interpersonal skills? If you hang around a major corporation for several years you will see the truth in this. If you're bright, have excellent "people" skills, and an innate drive toward continuous improvement, now is the time to begin leveraging these gifts by using Six Sigma concepts and methodologies. Rather than wait until you are given the level of leadership you've dreamed of, start now. Begin to show your supervisor and top management that you can:

- Build relationships with your direct reports based on trust, collaboration, and customer focus
- Inspire your staff to tackle root causes and improve processes through a more specific methodology
- Build a team that supports a common goal and philosophy and moves toward it

Relationship building is critical to successful implementation of Six Sigma concepts. It's obvious that some managers don't go out of their way to build a relationship with each of their direct reports; they don't believe this is what they get paid to do. Perhaps they feel that time spent getting to know their staff on a more personal level is not an efficient use of time. While we are hired to accomplish the goals at hand, the manager who doesn't particularly care how well he or she knows

Table 3.1   Why Your New Philosophy Will Benefit Your Staff

Key Concept	Benefits to Your Staff
Process Focus	Your staff will be able to contribute to process discussions and provide input to the processes they are responsible to perform. They will be respected for their valuable input. This builds self-esteem. Self-esteem inspires people to achieve their top potential.
Customer Focus	Your staff will feel the impact of becoming one of your key customers. That's right. You are providing a service to them by being their boss; they have critical needs that you must meet in order for them to reach their potential. In turn, you are also their customer. This mindset causes both you and your reports to gain a common understanding that each person plays a valuable role in the organization.
Collaboration	Your staff will see you as a leader and mentor rather than just a supervisor or boss when you make it a point to collaborate with them and coach them rather than strictly giving directives.
Data Driven Management	Just as having data to support your accomplishments will benefit you, it will benefit your staff. They can take ownership of the processes to which they are assigned, work to improve and control those processes, and eventually have the data to show what they've accomplished.
Strategic Planning	People feel more secure and can perform better when they know exactly what the goal is, what steps are necessary, and when each step is expected. Your staff will appreciate having Project Plans or team charters to support their day-to-day work.

the staff may not see the results hoped for or build a world-class organizational culture over time. Table 3.1 lists reasons why your staff will like your new Six Sigma-based philosophy.

Managers who embrace collaboration seek to create an atmosphere that encourages staff to contribute ideas and opinions without fear of repercussions. Collaboration begs for increased creativity and respect for individuals at all levels. In order to propagate collaboration within your personal organization, you first must be willing to collaborate with your staff. By doing so, you are showing them, by example, how to collaborate with their suppliers and customers. The size and scope of your personal organization will dictate the appropriate level and type of collaboration possible. For larger organizations, the best way to begin is to build a collaborative atmosphere among your direct reports. Tell them that collaboration is important and that it is one of the basic philosophies that you would like to see pushed down through *your* organization. When people genuinely enjoy working with you, they will accomplish more for you. This means a more productive staff and greater accomplishments for all. This is what makes you a leader as opposed to being a dime-a-dozen manager.

Regardless of your current scope or the size of your personal organization, implementing Six Sigma concepts will allow you to demonstrate strategic thinking. You don't need a particular headcount or responsibilities to be a strategic thinker. Even if you only manage yourself, carefully planning projects, working with others through customer focus and collaboration, and working toward a solid vision shows strategic planning. Strategy is figuring out how you will achieve a specific goal—whether it is to win a war, gain a promotion, improve quality, or get a date with the person in the next cubicle. Senior managers and executives are expected to set strategy for their organizations. By embracing Six Sigma concepts, you can step onto a clear path toward understanding and implementing strategic thinking, planning, and execution.

We cannot manage what we do not understand. This holds true for management of people, projects, and processes. Many managers believe that they can be successful, that they have gained the right to manage, based on their keen technical knowledge. However, it takes much more than an excellent understanding of regulations, a particular product, or the intricate details of specialized manufacturing equipment to rise above the management crowd. Managers at all levels who move ahead and end up with a top-notch résumé and consistently please senior management strive to understand the motivations of those whom they manage, the specific needs of their customers, and the processes that ultimately provide these people satisfaction.

Managers at all levels can improve performance through Six Sigma concepts and tools, incorporating applications more intrinsically into their world. By doing so, over time, quality can improve from the inside out rather than attacking from the outside in (e.g., consultants, Black Belts, etc.). This new perspective will also help middle management to work more collaboratively with Black Belts. In his book, *The Six Sigma Way*, Peter Pande tells us that a real Six Sigma organization is one that has taken up the challenge of measuring and improving *all* processes, with the objective of building that responsive, closed-loop system for business leadership or creating a culture of continuous improvement. In other words, simply using Six Sigma measures or a few tools does not qualify a company to be a "Six Sigma Organization." While it's true that in both large and small organizations, implementation of Six Sigma can be limited to the use of its tools for project facilitation, the opposite scenario, using Six Sigma as described by Pande, can occur on both large and small scales as well. In essence, if you and your direct reports are an "organization," Six Sigma concepts and tools can be incorporated into your management framework. As managers, we are tasked with managing, whether it is people or projects. In the end, there must be an outcome, an output that we are responsible to pass to the next person or group or organization. Let's begin to take the responsibility rather than wait for high-level support.

The skills you will gain and demonstrate through implementing Six Sigma methodologies and concepts in your own scope of work can be used as you seek out top management spots. Once you get there, you will be prepared to make the choices and decisions that drive the culture and bottom line results for the entire company.

When I first heard about Six Sigma, I was enthused by the promising results and equally humbled by the imperative that high-level support was needed for implementation. At the time, I was excited about being a new manager and was determined to develop a framework or strategy to ensure success for both my team and myself. I came back to work from my first business/quality conference determined to find ways to implement the basics without having to get an appointment with my CEO. Since then, I have successfully created a personal management framework based on Six Sigma concepts and have implemented this management style at several major pharmaceutical companies, including Novartis, Wyeth, and now Johnson & Johnson. I've hit roadblocks and have had to rally support from coworkers, staff, and supervisors. All things said and considered, I have seen great success in infusing the concepts deeper into each organization because in the business world, quality is contagious.

The Bottom Line

- Infusing the five basic concepts underlying Six Sigma and the associated methodologies and tools into your own organization will help you reach your professional goals.
- By streamlining your processes through implementing a Six Sigma-based process focus, you may be able to take on additional responsibilities by utilizing staff more efficiently.
- It will be easier to gain customer buy-in, when necessary, because you have taken the time to build strong relationships by following customer-focused and collaborative Six Sigma concepts.
- By implementing processes at the functional level that allow for data driven management, a key Six Sigma concept, you will create valuable business metrics to support the accomplishments of your team.
- Accomplishments are vague if not supported by data. Data supported results can help generate additional senior management support.
- If you're bright, have excellent "people" skills, and an innate drive toward continuous improvement, now is the time to begin leveraging these gifts by using Six Sigma concepts and methodologies.
- Managers at all levels who move ahead end up with top-notch résumés and consistently please senior management by striving to understand:

- The motivations of those whom they manage,
- The specific needs of their customers, and
- The processes that ultimately provide these people satisfaction.
- Six Sigma concepts and methodologies can provide a roadmap for success.

Part Two

Applying Six Sigma: A Manager's Perspective

Chapter 4

Creating a Personal Management Framework to Support Implementation of Six Sigma

Do not let what you cannot do interfere with what you can do.
—John Wooden, legendary UCLA basketball coach

To make a conscious decision about how you will manage your own organization, you will need to adopt a personal management framework. A *management framework* is a structure that allows or guides decisions—an organizational system, if you will, regardless of scope, that supports actions. On a personal level, it should comprise the management principles that drive your personal organization. If asked, could you immediately describe your management framework? I usually ask this question when interviewing managerial candidates. Over the years, the most common responses have been "I don't micromanage," "I have an open-door policy with employees," and "I maintain high standards for my employees." While these are all admirable statements, they do not constitute a strong framework that can drive results and impact culture. There are three key components to think about when developing a rock-solid management framework. These are:

1. What operational concepts/values/norms will serve as the day-to-day cornerstones for your personal organization, thus driving all interactions and decisions?
2. What is your vision for your personal organization—what would you like it to look like in five years?
3. What management style is important to you as the organizational leader?

This framework can be documented in any number of ways. It can be as simple as a list, or it can come in the form of an essay. For J&J, it is our credo. A strong *personal* management framework will impact the culture of *your* organization. Six Sigma organizations such as GE create a framework for their management using the key Six Sigma concepts. These Six Sigma concepts can also serve as day-to-day cornerstones for the manager's personal framework.

What operational concepts or values serve as the day-to-day cornerstones for your personal organization? What drives your interactions and decisions? At the root, Six Sigma operates under guiding principles that are similar to other major quality management philosophies such as the Baldrige Criteria, ISO 9000, Lean, and most other well-known quality management systems or philosophies. While each has its own spin and unique focus, the underlying concepts that can best be integrated into the manager's framework are the following.

Cornerstone 1: Process Focus

As managers, we can ensure that the processes falling within our scope are documented, communicated, measured, and continuously improved. In order to focus on process improvement, identify the core processes for which you are responsible. Basically, what do you get paid to do? The easiest way to identify your core processes is to identify *your* outputs or deliverables—not those of your broader organization. Within the scope of your work, the outputs are defined as anything that you or your direct reports are responsible to deliver to someone else or another group ("the customer"). This can range from a piece of data to an in-depth report. It can also be an object or one tiny geltab.

Each output should have an associated process that defines how it is generated. This is your core process, and it's distinct from support processes. Unlike core processes, support processes enable the successful delivery of the outputs. Examples include information systems, budgeting, and staff recruitment and hiring. A strong focus on core processes requires that you evaluate your own core processes and those of your reports on an ongoing basis, a daunting task when time and resources are limited. It's easy to fall into the habit of focusing, instead, on "on-time" delivery. However, if you shift your focus to the underlying process, you will reap the benefits of removing inefficiencies while improving quality. Don't expect to be able to do this all at once. Sometimes, this process may require a temporary "slowdown" period, during which you reevaluate what you're doing, why you're doing it, and what it means for your customers.

The DMAIC cycle drives Six Sigma process improvements. Traditional Six Sigma programs driven by top management directives, Six Sigma Champions, and Black Belts work closely with functional managers to understand, improve, and maintain successful processes using Six Sigma tools. However, self-empowered managers can follow the same directives, as shown in Table 4.1.

Table 4.1   Process Improvement
Six Sigma DMAIC for Middle Managers

DMAIC Stage	Traditional Six Sigma with High-Level Support	Self-Empowered Middle Managers
Define	The Six Sigma Champion and Executive Council identify, evaluate, and select potential projects. They prepare a problem and mission statement and a team charter. They select and kick-off teams.	As the Manager/Champion, you can identify, evaluate, and select "Problem or Improvement Projects" for your staff and work with them to ensure that they understand the issues and your mission. These problems or opportunities for improvement can be documented in a Project Plan. For a larger staff (i.e., 20 or more), team charters can be developed. You are the Champion of your personal organization.
Measure	The Six Sigma Project Team measures a baseline performance, then maps and measures the problem process. They determine what to measure and how to collect the data.	You can work with your staff to map out the process and collect baseline performance data. Then you can determine what metrics should be measured and how the data will be collected. Remember to keep it simple!
Analyze	The Six Sigma Project Team analyzes the "as-is" process and the variables within the process by using the data collected.	You or a designee can analyze the "as-is" process, determining where there may be gaps, unnecessary hand-offs, etc. In discussing how to improve the process, you can evaluate value-added versus non-value-added steps and options for process improvement. Your team can also analyze baseline data.
Improve	The Six Sigma Project Team with the Operating Group (middle manager and staff) plans designed experiments. They determine how to optimize process performance, evaluate potential improvements, and implement improvements.	Once you have determined the best process based on the data you have tracked, you can diagram and pilot the new process.
Control	The Six Sigma Project Team and the Operating Group documents improved processes, implements them, and monitors them.	You can document and implement the improved process. Then you can continue to track appropriate metrics to determine whether the process is holding up over time. If your data demonstrates a "dip" in performance, you can investigate and take appropriate action.

Cornerstone 2: Customer Focus

Six Sigma is all about the customer. Each person or group that accepts an output from you is your personal customer. Customer focus requires that you strive to understand the customers' specifications or needs constantly. Attitude is key! When you understand that your job is to deliver the most accurate rendition of what the customer desires, working relationships become more positive, collaboration improves, and barriers and silos begin to break down because goals start to merge. Individual agendas move toward the center, paving the way for an increase in creative solutions, processes, and win-win situations. This is not to say that the manager must forgo all reason to meet customer needs, but managers should keep their internal and external customers in mind at all times.

Business and process decisions should always tie back to customer needs, and each step of any process should always add value for your customer. For example, if your team is filing a particular Quality Assurance form in two places, why are they? Is this a value-added activity? Does it benefit your internal and external customers? To ask these questions, you must have a clear understanding of who your customers are and you must talk to them.

Cornerstone 3: Collaboration

The Six Sigma philosophy calls for collaboration to expose processes fully and generate the best outcomes. Only through collaboration can managers determine if their piece of a larger process is meeting customer requirements. If you are willing to collaborate with suppliers and customers, you'll find they have a wellspring of ideas that can help you add value to your core processes. Often, suppliers and customers already have ideas about what you should be doing. Just ask them!

Cornerstone 4: Data Driven Management

In Six Sigma, since decisions are based on data and facts, it is essential to collect and evaluate appropriate metrics. Any measurement that helps managers understand its processes and operations is a potential business metric. Some examples are number of units completed per hour, percentage of defects or errors for a process, and hours required to deliver a certain number of units. You can begin the process of managing by data by identifying deliverables and understanding what the customer values. Managers can track value-added metrics to ensure that customer needs are being met and to support decisions about processes, people, and projects.

You should learn about and use standard Six Sigma tools such as Pareto charts, histograms, control charts, and flowcharts, as appropriate. Many of these tools have been around for a while and are fairly easy to use. If deliverables are measured in ways that are meaningful to both you and your customer, discussions rooted in fact can occur and proper decisions will be made by both parties. Don't underestimate the power of numbers coupled with excellent customer focus. Determining appropriate measures or metrics for each key deliverable is critical. When determining which metrics are value-added, managers should first consider the amount of time it will take to record and analyze the metrics relative to the value it will add. The general rule: "Keep it simple."

Cornerstone 5: Strategic Planning

You can strategically plan activities that ensure data-supported quality deliverables. If you cannot personally roll out Six Sigma to your entire organization with the aid of your CEO and his team, you can begin to embrace these concepts and incorporate them into your day-to-day work.

Once committed, you will need to develop a strategy for how you can introduce this new focus on the Six Sigma concepts to your direct reports—your own organization. The ease of determining the value of metrics increases with your understanding of the outcome you are working toward. To create a strategy, goals must be clearly defined and understood. Understanding the big picture, the vision, is critical to determining what metrics are important to track and which are not. There should be a reason for why someone is spending time to record and analyze metrics. The purpose may be to:

- Show that a new process is superior to the old
- Ensure that customer specifications are met
- Test several approaches and determine which is best
- Access productivity against process and other organizational changes

There are numerous reasons why particular metrics are useful, but if you do not clearly understand the desired outcome, you risk wasting valuable time recording data that is not useful in the end.

Do you have a clear vision of what you would like your personal organization to look like in five years? As you create a personal management framework and set strategy to inspire staff while accomplishing your goals, you should know that there are only two known sources that can inspire the energy needed to transform an organization, including yours. They are crisis and vision. Many companies begin a quality management program as a reaction to a crisis. I have observed this situation first hand in several pharmaceutical companies with regard to top management support of both quality and compliance related initiatives. Once the company is inspected by a regulatory agency and falls short, the crisis is in full swing. Throughout my 17 years in the industry, it continues to amaze me that pharmaceutical companies are still slow to learn from one another. A few crises that have hit pharmaceutical companies over the last few years are:

- Wyeth received an FDA warning letter because of manufacturing inspection results.
- Wyeth stock dropped dramatically when studies showed that hormone replacement might not be the healthiest option for menopausal women.
- A counterfeit version of a major J & J product, Procrit, was being sold on the market.
- Pfizer received an FDA warning letter for their drug safety reporting practices.

Of course, all of these issues caused top management to swing heavily in the direction of change.

A method to incite change is to create a crisis by evaluating the organization in various ways to forecast future issues. In other words, vision can be created to offset forecasted crisis! It is referred to as "creating a crisis" to signify the level of commitment required to propel the vision across the organization. Two methods used to create a crisis are (1) seeking to understand the needs of customers and (2) brainstorming about what crises a particular industry, company, or functional area is facing. Creation of a crisis is consistent with change management principles. The task of managing change includes both the making of changes in a planned and managed or systematic fashion and the response to changes over which the organization exercises little or no control (e.g., legislation, social and political upheaval, the actions of competitors, shifting economic tides and currents, and so on). Making changes in a planned and managed or systematic fashion usually refers to changes that lie within and are controlled by the organization. Researchers and practitioners alike typically distinguish between a knee-jerk or reactive response (from a crisis) and an anticipative or proactive response. As the Champion of your own organization, you can inspire an anticipative or proactive response by creating a crisis of your own. If you choose to create a crisis, you must follow through with an appropriate vision for your personal organization. A vision can replace the crisis as a rallying point for the promotion of the Six Sigma cornerstone concepts outlined above. At the heart of change management lies the change problem—that is, some future state to be realized, some current state to be left behind, and some structured, organized process for getting from one to the other. This embodies the concept of creating a crisis because the implication is that management will identify the critical needed change and then move forward to carry their organization to a new and better state where the root of the crisis no longer exists.

Transformational change often occurs only when a series of events external to the organization cause people at all levels to examine their basic assumptions. The time to begin changing is before a competitive or other type of crisis emerges. When an organization is in a position of strength, resources are available to support the change and time is on the side of the organization. By the time a crisis is recognized, it's difficult, and sometimes impossible, to regain a meaningful competitive advantage. Creating a crisis is a way for managers to honestly assess what issues are facing them prior to an unwelcome slap in the face. They can proactively create the crisis when they are strong in order to position their organization and avoid a true crisis situation. For middle managers, a crisis can be any number of things, depending on the focus, deliverables, goal, and objectives of their personal organizations.

Creating crisis is good in that it supports a proactive approach, forecasting, if you will, crises before they occur. Also important is sustaining that vision long term. Vision can "move" an organization to change, but true, unwavering leadership is required to sustain such a push. True leaders embrace their message. They are driven in their approach to making positive changes. This is critical to implementing a new management framework based on the Six Sigma cornerstone concepts. It sounds quite simple, but it is often difficult. Managers must be able to spread their heartfelt vision to staff, supervisors, and as many other leaders as possible within the organization. This is done both overtly, at meetings and in business interactions, and in subtle ways, such as facial expressions and gestures. The words and how they are said must match the vision that has been communicated to all employees. Sometimes the part about how thing are said is the most difficult.

What management style is important to you as the organizational leader? The late Dr. W. Edward Deming (1900–1993), one of the foremost experts in quality control in the United States, had a profound impact on Japanese industry after being invited to speak to the Japan Medical Association. Through a series of seminars, Dr. Deming taught the basics of statistical quality control plainly and thoroughly to executives, managers, engineers, and researchers of Japanese industries.

W. Edward Deming's theory of management is yet another quality management basic that supports Six Sigma concepts and methodologies. Deming's 14 points for management, published in 1980, condense his theory and provide a roadmap for leaders who want to transform their organizations. His theory is based on understanding the difference between common and special cause variation. Managers should realize that unless a change is made to the system (which only they can make), the system's capability will remain the same. This capability is determined by common variation, which is inherent in any system. Just as our weight is not exactly the same each day, there are small inherent systemic changes that take place within systems. Employees can't control a common cause of variation and shouldn't be held accountable for, or penalized for, its outcomes. Common variation can be caused by factors such as poor lighting, lack of ongoing job-skill training, or poor product design. On the other hand, new raw materials, a broken machine part, or a new employee can cause special variation; it's situational. This emphasis on common and special cause variation is a key focus of Six Sigma methodology when determining how to improve processes.

Deming's 14 points apply to organizations of all sizes and in all industries, both manufacturing and nonmanufacturing. They apply to your functional area. Table 4.2 demonstrates the 14 points and how they apply to the middle manager's unique goals.

Deming's 14 Points for Management

Table 4.2   Deming in Action

Deming's Points for Management	Applied to Middle Management
1. Create constancy of purpose toward improvement and service, with the aim to become competitive and to stay in business, and to provide jobs.	Constancy of purpose with an aim to become competitive and stay in business is critical in any functional area. Companies are downsizing and restructuring more than ever. Your personal organization must add undisputable value to the overall organization!
2. Adopt the new philosophy. We are in a new economic age. Western management must awaken to the challenge, must learn their responsibilities, and take on leadership for change.	This refers to embracing quality management concepts into the management mainstream. By reading this book, you are demonstrating your interest in these concepts. Now you must adopt them in your day-to-day world. Take on the responsibility instead of waiting for a Six Sigma Black Belt!
3. Cease dependence on inspection to achieve quality. Eliminate the need for inspection on a mass basis by building quality into the product in the first place.	Managers should create a process-focused organization that builds quality into products and deliverables at every step.
4. End the practice of awarding business on the basis of price tag. Instead, minimize total cost. Move toward a single supplier for any one item, on a long-term relationship of loyalty and trust.	Going back to inputs and outputs, this point drives home the need for maintaining high standards for your own organization and those of your suppliers. Where possible, develop relationships of loyalty and trust with your suppliers. Collaborate!
5. Improve constantly and forever the system of production and service to improve quality and productivity, and thus constantly decrease costs.	Remember the quote by Will Rogers! Don't just stay in the same place forever, as a manager or as a person, and don't allow your processes and products to remain constant. Improve constantly!
6. Institute training on the job.	Place value on staff training. Allow staff the time to attend training sessions and/or relevant conferences. Support continuing education.

Deming's Points for Management	Applied to Middle Management
7. Institute leadership. The aim of supervision should be to help people and machines and gadgets to do a better job. Supervision of management is in need of overhaul, as well as supervision of production workers.	Be a leader not a dictator. Develop that collaborative and creative culture within your personal organization that naturally moves all involved toward new levels of achievement.
8. Drive out fear, so that everyone may work effectively for the company.	Treat your staff, customers, suppliers, stakeholders, and colleagues with respect. View these individuals as your personal customers. Particularly with staff, this will drive out fear of failure, repercussions, and miscommunication, paving the way for more symbiotic relationships that create fantastic results.
9. Break down barriers between departments. People in research, design, sales, and production must work as a team to foresee issues that may be encountered with the product or service.	Collaborate! Collaborate! Collaborate! Maintain a strong customer focus at all times.
10. Eliminate slogans, exhortations, and targets for the workforce asking for zero defects and new levels of productivity. Such exhortations only create adversarial relationships, as the bulk of the causes of low quality and low productivity belong to the system and thus lie beyond the power of the workforce.	Focus on quality of deliverables rather than meeting timelines while sacrificing quality. Base organization decisions on this concept so that human resources are balanced with workload. Engage the workforce in finding creative solutions. Focus on alleviating root causes of low productivity rather than assuming people are not working hard enough.
11. Eliminate work standards (quotas) on the factory floor. Substitute leadership. Eliminate management by objective. Eliminate management by numbers and numerical goals. Substitute leadership.	This point refers to quotas that may be in place for productivity not value-added business metrics. It also refers to engaging workers with true leadership causing them to want to produce for you rather than tossing them directives as to the level of productivity you expect day to day.
12. Remove barriers that rob the hourly worker of his or her right to pride of workmanship. The responsibility of supervisors must be changed from sheer numbers to quality. Remove barriers that rob people in management and in engineering of their right to pride of workmanship. This means, *inter alia*, abolishment of the annual or merit rating and of management by objective.	Elimination of the annual merit rating is unthinkable to many big US companies; however these points can be applied in the following way within your own organization: • Consider *how* a person accomplished his or her goals, not just if the goal was accomplished. • Delegate responsibilities to staff that allow them to take pride in their work—give them ownership.

(Continues)

Table 4.2   *(Continued)*

Deming's Points for Management	Applied to Middle Management
	• Base yearly reviews not only on the quantity that was delivered, but also on the quality of deliverables and the resulting impact to your organization, to the customers, and to suppliers in your work chain.
13. Institute a vigorous program of education and self-improvement.	Just as you should strive for continuous improvement of your processes, continuously improve yourself. Embrace growth. Do not allow yourself to grow stagnant.
14. Put everybody in the company to work to accomplish the transformation. The transformation is everybody's job.	Develop a strategy to infuse your new management framework by including the Six Sigma cornerstone concepts into your personal organization. Get everyone involved and reward involvement!

In creating a management framework, I suggest choosing three of Deming's 14 points as the most important. These can then be combined with the five cornerstone concepts of Six Sigma and your personal vision to create an individualized framework. For me, choosing three of the 14 points was difficult, but after much consideration, I choose the following:

- Improve constantly and forever the system of production and service to improve quality and productivity, and thus constantly decrease costs.
- Institute leadership. The aim of leadership should be to help people and machines and gadgets to do a better job. Leadership of management is in need of overhaul, as well as leadership of production workers.
- Drive out fear, so that everyone may work effectively for the company.

My choices are based on my experience, the type of work I do, and the issues that face my industry.

Improve Constantly and Forever the System of Production and Service to Improve Quality and Productivity, and Constantly Decrease Costs

I believe this is a critical point for every industry. No matter how good you are, even if you're Number 1, something better can come along. I believe that organizations that do not look forward at all times to see how they can continue to improve are like a person who thinks he or she is perfect. It is commonly known that nobody is perfect. I believe it should be commonly accepted, even in *Fortune* 100 companies, that no company is perfect. There should be a degree of humility on the part of top management that feeds a continuous push to improve. There are numerous examples of companies that became complacent and lost market share (such as General Motors) or even shut their doors. Also, as stated in this book, as the world around organizations changes, so should the organization. There are many drivers (such as economic climate, pop culture, environmental changes, grass roots campaigns, increased sophistication of customers, etc.) that impact the success of an organization or the demand for a particular product. All of these influence success and cannot be ignored.

Institute Leadership

The aim of leadership should be to help people and machines and gadgets to do a better job. Leadership of management is in need of overhaul, as well as leadership of production workers. Some examples of the problems associated with management by results include:

- Systems of controls without a long-term, larger purpose will always set up conflict in an organization.
- When measurable controls are unattainable or impractical, individuals and groups tend to fabricate conformance.
- The charade of conformance fosters guarded communications and minor—and even major—dishonesty.
- The inevitable contradictions among the controls of different departments leads to finger pointing, blame games, and an endless series of excuses like "If it weren't for them..."
- Behind the worst shortcomings of management by results is fear.

Realizing these problems, people wonder what a better alternative is. I believe that Deming's point on leadership is critical because it is the answer to this question. True leadership places focus on giving top value to customers by building excellence into every aspect of the organization. This is done by creating an environment that allows and encourages everyone to contribute to the organization and by developing the skills that enable them to scientifically study and constantly improve every process by which work is accomplished. A true leader leads in a way that makes people want to follow by his or her treatment of them, belief in them, and support of them. People will follow a true leader to the ends of the Earth (our most frightening example being Hitler). Management by results hinders the leader from reaching his or her full potential as a leader because there is always that element of fear (my next choice for the top three of Deming's 14 points).

Management by leadership places an emphasis on studying processes and on executing them better and better to provide customers with products and services of ever-increasing value at ever-lower costs. This philosophy starts with the customer, not with the bottom line profit and loss statement. There is freedom and creativity, yet there is control. There is the freedom to discover new markets, to develop new systems, to gain greater mastery over the processes. And there is the control of a data-based approach to improvement. When quality is increased by improving processes (not by expanded inspection), the improved quality will lead to improved productivity. This leads to lower costs, which lead to lower prices. Better quality and lower prices mean the company can expand its market and can stay in business creating jobs and a greater return on investment. Management by results, on the other hand, tends to focus only on the end result: the return on investment. It is like wagging the tail to keep a dog healthy.

Drive Out Fear, So That Everyone May Work Effectively for the Company

Deming said, "People are entitled to joy in their work and a sense of ownership." I firmly believe that my staff is more productive when I support a culture of teamwork and respect. I focus on the talents of individuals. As I stated above, nobody is perfect. Why should I put expectations on people that they cannot meet? We have team goals to improve our processes, and we work together to accomplish them. We each play an important role, and we need one another to be successful.

Fear can invite wrong figures. Bearers of bad news fare badly. To keep a job or just to keep in favor, an employee may present to his or her boss only good news. Fear is insidious and may not be overtly recognizable, but the concept is ever present in management by results and impacts the organizational culture. Management by results does not support a culture of honesty and teamwork. It is very difficult to impact change in this area because a paradigm shift is needed.

I encourage you to consider your current management framework: whether it exists, whether you can describe it, and whether there may be a more powerful one waiting for you as you close the back cover of this book. Developing such a framework is key to implementing Six Sigma concepts into your day-to-day work—and making it work.

The Bottom Line

- A management framework is a structure that allows or guides decisions, an organizational system, if you will, regardless of the scope that supports actions. It comprises the management principles that drive your personal organization.
- Six Sigma organizations such as GE create frameworks for their management by using the key Six Sigma concepts. The concepts can also serve as day-to-day cornerstones for the manager's personal framework.

- The three key components to think about when developing a strong management framework are
  - What operational concepts/values/norms will serve as the day-to-day cornerstones for your personal organization, thus driving all interactions and decisions?
  - What is your vision for your personal organization? What would you like it to look like in five years?
  - What management style is important to you as the organizational leader?
- As you create a personal management framework and set strategy to inspire staff while accomplishing your goals, you should know that there are only two known sources that can inspire the energy needed to transform an organization, including yours. They are crisis and vision.
- A method to incite change is to create a crisis by evaluating the organization in various ways to forecast future issues. Two methods used to create a crisis are (1) seeking to understand the needs of customers, and (2) brainstorming about what crises the particular industry, company, or functional area are facing.
- W. Edward Deming's theory of management is yet another quality management basic that supports Six Sigma concepts and methodologies. Deming's 14 points for management, published in 1980, condense his theory and provide a roadmap for leaders who want to transform their organizations. His points should be considered when developing a personal management framework.

Chapter 5

Focusing on Process

Excellence is to do a common thing in an uncommon way.
—Booker T. Washington

Essentially, all Six Sigma activities, concepts, and tools revolve around the DMAIC model. The DMAIC methodology serves to *define* a process to improve, *measure* the baseline and target performance of the process, *analyze* process data to determine the key process inputs that affect outputs, *improve* the process to optimize outputs, and, finally, *control* the improved process. Middle managers can apply the same methodology and focus on process to improve efficiency and effectiveness of their personal organizations.

Within the Johnson & Johnson (J&J) Medicines & Nutritionals Group, the Benefit Risk Management (BRM) organization serves a corporate function for drug safety surveillance or pharmacovigilance. BRM is the organization within the J&J Pharmaceuticals Group that is responsible for accepting reports of adverse events (side effects) from a variety of sources, including healthcare professionals and consumers. We are responsible for evaluating individual adverse event cases as well as aggregate data to access the safety of our products on an ongoing basis. Examples from BRM will be used to demonstrate how managers can apply a process focus. BRM is comprised of approximately 400 employees and includes multiple functions. It represents a medium-sized organization within the context of J&J. The concepts described below and, in some cases, demonstrated in examples from J&J can also be applied to smaller and larger organizations. Of course, applying Six Sigma to an entire company should follow the traditional Six Sigma methodologies and strategies, which are well described in the current literature.

Table 5.1 Process-Focused Activities within the DMAIC Model

DMAIC Stage	Process Activity	Deliverable(s)
Define	Identify key organizational deliverables Identify process to improve Map high-level process	Problem statement Process/Project scope Initial SIPOC with high-level process, defined scope, inputs, and outputs
Measure	Identify process inputs and outputs	SIPOC for process
Analyze	Map the "as-is" process Brainstorm about the process Analyze the process flow Create detailed "to-be" process map	Detailed "as-is" process map Process Flow Analysis Detailed "to-be" process map
Improve	Pilot process change(s)	Updated process maps Pilot run information/learning
Control	Institutionalize improvement	Standard Operating Procedures

Table 5.1 demonstrates the critical role processes play within the DMAIC model by showing some of the key, straightforward process activities that can be applied by managers, as well as the resulting outputs. Similar tables outlining the key activities related to the cornerstone concepts of customer focus and collaboration and data driven management will be provided in Chapters 6 and 7, respectively. You will notice that many of the activities involve more than one of the cornerstone concepts. However, they have been categorized based on how the activity can best demonstrate the concepts. Chapter 8 will bring together all the activities and deliverables from Chapters 5 through 7 to clarify how you can create a realistic, strategy for implementing Six Sigma in your daily work that best fits your business goals, environment, and availability considering all your responsibilities.

Focusing on Process during the Define Stage

Understanding the process-related activities and deliverables and why these are important will help you achieve the goal of implementing Six Sigma.

DMAIC Stage	Process Activity	Deliverable(s)
Define	Identify key organizational deliverables Identify process to improve Map high-level process	Problem statement Process/Project scope Initial SIPOC with high-level process, defined scope, inputs, and outputs

Identification of Key Organizational Outputs

To identify a process to improve, you must first have a clear understanding of the processes for which you are responsible. Even more basic is the understanding of what constitutes a process. What exactly is a *process*? Arthur Tenner and Irving DeToro provide a great definition of process in their book, *Process Redesign: The Implementation Guide for Managers:* "One or more tasks that add value by transforming a set of inputs into a specified set of outputs (good or services) for another person (customer) by a combination of people, methods, and tools."

Understanding where to find processes and their boundaries within your personal organization is a critical step. Being clear on the boundaries within which you have to work is particularly important if you are interested in implementing Six Sigma in a company that does not have a traditional Six Sigma program in place. Many jobs or industries have processes that are easily identified; they are more visible in that they are formally documented and are constantly refined. Examples of highly visible process are found in manufacturing, pharmaceuticals, medicine, and the aircraft industry. If you work in a regulated industry, particularly one that requires process documentation, you probably have a jump-start in the process focus area. In this case, the key may be identifying the "part" of the process that you own. This will be your scope. If your personal organization owns the entire process, you are in a position to more fully evaluate and impact the entire process: you have a larger process scope. However, it is important to note that just because a process is documented doesn't mean that it is a good process, a valuable process, or a cost effective one.

Jobs or industries such as the professional services practiced by attorneys or accountants may have fewer documented processes. Their processes may be less obvious, or invisible, by definition. Regardless of visibility, in all cases where an output is generated, a process or series of processes was used to produce a product or to deliver a service.

As noted in Chapter 2, when applying Six Sigma concepts to your own scope of work, I recommend that you begin by identifying key outputs for which your group is responsible. Depending on the size and complexity of your personal organization, you will need to drill down through the big picture toward the detail. Remember that your personal outputs are identified by what you hand off to another person or group within your company. Your personal outputs, in the majority of cases, will not be an end product of the company.

Johnson & Johnson Example

The following key internal and external outputs were identified in order to develop a metrics program for the BRM Division within the Johnson & Johnson Medicines & Nutritionals Group:

- Individual adverse event cases and the applicable regulatory forms for submission to regulatory agencies
- Aggregate adverse event data listings generated from our computer system
- Finalized aggregate adverse event reports required by regulations or requested by our internal customers such as:
  - Investigational New Drug (IND) Annual Reports required by the Food and Drug Administration (FDA)
  - New Drug Development (NDA) Periodic Reports required by the FDA
  - Periodic Safety Update Reports required by the European Medicines Agency (EMEA)
  - Benefit Risk Assessment Reports
  - Epidemiology Reports
  - Trend Reports
  - Various specialized pharmacovigilance reports requested by regulatory agencies as well as by other J&J groups or organizations

This list was generated by brainstorming about what items we produce and hand over to another J&J group or to external requestors. BRM has other types of outputs, but these are the standard outputs that serve as the most critical ones and take up the majority of the organization's time and effort to generate. From the list of key outputs, a list of core processes was generated:

- Processing and evaluation of individual adverse event cases
- Global distribution of processed serious adverse event cases for submission to local regulatory agencies
- Submission of spontaneous expedited adverse event reports to the FDA and EMEA
- Evaluation of aggregate adverse event data
- Identification of adverse events published in the literature
- Identification and analysis of safety trends and signals

To clarify, we also identified key processes that are considered support processes only. These are different from core processes in that they provide the necessary tools and structure to complete the core processes, thereby generating the key outputs of the organization. BRM has many support processes. Some of the major ones are:

- Regulatory compliance—Processes ensuring that the company is meeting all laws and legal obligations
- Information systems—Technical movement and processing of data and information to expedite business operations and decisions
- Quality management—Systems and activities to ensure effective, high-quality execution of the work of the business

- Budgeting—Processes for deciding how funds will be allocated over a period of time
- Recruitment and hiring—Acquisition of people to do the work of the division
- Evaluation and compensation—Assessment and payment of people for the work/value they provide to the division
- Contract management—Processes to ensure appropriate contracts are in place to ensure that the work of the division can proceed in an effective and compliant manner
- Regulatory liaison—Activities ensuring that the division is adequately informed of the external environment including regulatory changes and opinions

It may be that you are responsible for a support process within an organization, or you may be a manager or director responsible for one of the core processes within your larger organization. For example, you may be responsible for training, or all technical aspects within an organization, or all report writing. If so, the same concepts and methods for identifying key outputs and processes hold true. The key is assessing and understanding the scope for which you are responsible. It is within that scope that you can make an impact, regardless of whether or not your company has a traditional Six Sigma program in place.

Developing a Project Charter or Plan

Six Sigma projects begin with a Project Charter. Before you can develop a Project Charter or Plan, you must first select a process to improve. To choose a process on which to focus your attention, all you need to do is examine your list of core processes. The beauty of Six Sigma methodology is that it can be used to evaluate and improve any process. Again, for you, the key is scope. Creating a SIPOC for your chosen process will help you clarify the process scope as applied to your personal organization and the amount of process changes and activities over which you have influence.

The Project Charter generally includes the business case, a problem or opportunity statement, a goal statement, and the project scope. My favorite template is the DMAIC Project Charter Worksheet found in *The Six Sigma Way Team Fieldbook* by Peter Pande, Robert Neuman, and Roland Cavanagh. The charter can also identify the team leader, team members, key stakeholders, and milestones. Identification of these key elements early on is critical to project success. It allows the team to clarify and formalize their agreement and mutual understanding of the project. If your personal organization is large enough to warrant formation of teams, a Project Charter is an easy, quick tool that is value-added.

Considering all the other responsibilities you may have, you can reduce the time spent on this activity by limiting the charter to goals, scope, and business case, as appropriate. It may not be practical to spend too much time hashing out the perfect problem statement if the problem is very specific to your personal organization and everyone understands what that problem is. This is a judgment call on your part and depends on the size of your personal organization and the scope and complexity of the process you have decided to tackle. Many times, people get bogged down in creating a perfect Project Charter document when the more important point is to have a common understanding of why the project is important to the business (business case), what the main problem that you are aiming to resolve is (problem statement), what the main goal of the project is (goal statement), what the scope is, and who cares (the stakeholders). One advantage of using this tool within your own scope is that, in most cases, all those involved will already have a shared understanding of the issues and goals. This is in contrast to a cross-organizational project or a project that requires external consultants or Six Sigma Black Belts who do not have functional expertise equal to that of yourself and your reports. In traditional Six Sigma, the business case is normally handed down from the Champion or senior management. When working within your own organization, you are the Champion and should therefore understand the business case for the project on which you would like your team, staff, or individual contributor to focus. Goal statements similar to yearly goals set for employees should be written. Therefore, the goal statement should always include a description of what's to be accomplished, a measurable target, and a projected completion date.

If your personal organization is very small or if you have processes that are the sole responsibility of one person, each person can develop a simplified Project Charter or Project Plan that includes key details for completion of individual projects. At a minimum, the Project Plan should include the project goal, business case, and milestones. This will allow you and your employees to gain a common understanding of their individual projects and to come to an agreement. If the timing is right, yearly goals can be translated into project goals for your staff.

Within my personal organization at J&J, each of my direct reports is responsible for creating a Project Charter or Plan for his or her assignment that includes the evaluation, update, or creation of a process. Table 5.2 is the template that we use. There are many great templates, and again, which template you use is not the main concern. The concern is creating an avenue for shared understanding of the goal and how it will be achieved.

Creating a SIPOC for the Process

A SIPOC (suppliers, inputs, process, outputs, and customers) diagram is a quick and easy way to help identify the suppliers, inputs, outputs, and customers for each

Table 5.2 Global Quality Management: Project Charter/Plan

Responsible Person(s):		Business Case:		
Project Goal(s):				
Milestone #	**Key Milestones & Associated Actions**	**Comments**	**Due Date**	**Date Completed**
1.0				
	1.1			
	1.2			
2.0				
	2.1			
	2.2			
3.0				
	3.1			
	3.2			

of your key processes. A SIPOC can be helpful in identifying the boundaries of a process and the critical elements without getting into too much detail. It helps keep focus on the big picture when trying to identify the key deliverables and customers for the chosen process. When developing a problem or opportunity statement related to your chosen process, strive to focus on real problems that are directly related to cost, productivity and compliance, if applicable. Analyzing these elements of your process will be key activities during the analysis phase.

There are numerous templates for SIPOCs that can be used. Again, the point is not to create the most elaborate *visual* but to understand all the elements. Working within your own organization will go a long way toward completing these initial activities that much faster. Remember that these are activities that you should be able to do within your personal organization without necessarily having to obtain high-level support. That means that the activities should be kept as simple as possible while achieving a valuable result. For example, depending on your level of responsibility, it may or may not be possible to hold a full day off-site meeting to accomplish these tasks.

Advantages of creating a SIPOC are:

- Defining the scope within which you and your personal organization can impact the process; if you own the entire process, you will still need to define the process scope in terms of whether you will focus on the entire process or just a part of the process
- Defining the suppliers and their inputs
- Defining the outputs and the internal and external customers
- Creating a starting point for developing a detailed process map

Developing a SIPOC is a valuable activity to complete as a team. It is also helpful to have individuals create a SIPOC for the processes for which they are responsible.

Johnson & Johnson Example

The SIPOC created for the BRM core process of processing and evaluating individual adverse event cases is shown in Table 5.3. Identification of Suppliers and Customers will be discussed in Chapter 6, and the SIPOC example will be completed.

At this stage, the process should be condensed to from five to seven key steps. Process steps should be conveyed using action words. The steps should be listed as they occur today. Bearing all this in mind, the SIPOC provides a high-level perspective of the process. As the scope is critical, it is a good idea to add the process boundaries to the SIPOC as shown previously. All involved in the project should agree on the SIPOC content.

Focusing on Process during the Measure Stage

The main process-focused activity in the Measure Stage is that of identifying the inputs and outputs for your process and adding them to the SIPOC. This is categorized as a measurement activity because defining the outputs and inputs leads to identifying process metrics in order to manage the process using data. In addition, identifying and ensuring a mutual understanding of the inputs and outputs lead to proper identification of suppliers and customers.

DMAIC Stage	Process Activity	Deliverable(s)
Measure	Identify process inputs and outputs	Completed SIPOC for process

Per ISO 9000, a business adopts a process approach when it systematically identifies and manages its processes, particularly the interactions of those processes. Going a step further, the latest version of ISO 9000 requires that businesses

Table 5.3 J&J BRM Example SIPOC

Process:	Processing and evaluating of individual adverse event cases
Start Boundary:	Adverse event case is received by BRM
End Boundary:	Adverse event case is "promoted" in the computer system for worldwide distribution

Supplier(s)	Input(s)	PROCESS	Output(s)	Customer(s)
	Adverse event source documentation (raw data)	Receive and sort adverse event cases Register cases into computer system Process case data through the computer system Determine whether the adverse event is expected or not based on approved labeling Perform medical review of the case Perform quality control review Promote case for regulatory reporting	Processed data Regulatory forms	

think through the life cycle of a product in terms of small, interrelated processes. It highlights how one process affects the quality of the next. In a process-focused environment, staff members are trained to think in terms of how their work affects the quality of the processes that follow. This results in an ongoing push for high-quality input and output each time processes intersect and benefits both internal and external customer needs.

The most straightforward way to identify the inputs and outputs is to brainstorm about what is handed to your group at the start boundary of your process and then brainstorm about what is handed to the next individual, group, or organization at the end boundary of your process. It is not a difficult exercise in most cases but may be more challenging in organizations that have less-visible or invisible processes. For example, perhaps your deliverable is a service. Completion of the output section may be tricky; however, exploring and discussing what the output actually is will go a long way toward driving home Six Sigma thinking.

Focusing on Process during the Analyze Stage

DMAIC Stage	Process Activity	Deliverable(s)
Analyze	Map the "as-is" process Brainstorm about the process Analyze the process flow Create detailed "to-be" process map	Detailed "as-is" process map Process Flow Analysis Detailed "to-be" process map

Creating a Detailed "As-Is" Process Map

In the define stage, it is critical to understand the "as-is" process. A flowchart can be created to show the process details to analyze gaps, unnecessary handoffs, and inefficient practices. Once the "as-is" flowchart is created, gaps can be explored and addressed to create a "to-be" process. If possible, it is best to create flowcharts using software; however paper and pencil is a good place to start. My favorite software for creating flowcharts is Microsoft Visio. Whether you expect an individual responsible for a particular process to create the "as-is" flowchart or you expect a group or team of people in your personal organization to create it, starting on paper is best. At a minimum, sketching the process flow on paper is an extremely useful visual to aid discussions about even minor processes. For a group, a great method to use is what I call the "Sticky Note Method."

Sticky Note Method for Developing an "As-Is" Process Map

1. Tape flip chart paper onto the wall.
2. Be sure that you have already identified the starting boundary of your process, brainstorm to identify detailed steps in the process.
3. Designate one person to be the process step recorder. That person should write down all the actions that are discussed on sticky notes, recording only one action on each sticky note.
4. Next, have the recorder stick the actions on the flipchart paper. Then, as a group, order the action steps the way they happen today.
5. Draw arrows between the action steps indicating the process flow.
6. Also designate who completes each action and record it on the sticky note.

7. If there are steps in which a question must be answered to decide the next action, have the recorder write the question inside a triangle on a sticky note. When placed on the flip chart, this "triangle" should then have a "yes" direction and a "no" direction.

8. Be sure to include any situations where there is a loop in the process. This will usually include a question (as noted in number 7 above), but sometimes there is a double check or recheck for something.

When creating this process, strive to be as detailed as possible. Depending on the complexity of your process, this activity could take half an hour or a couple of hours. Again, this activity should not take so much time that you require "approval" from above. This is an example of how you, as an empowered manager, can require that your own organization explore and gain an in-depth understanding of the processes for which it is responsible. For organizations that have less-visible or invisible processes, this may be an insightful exercise. Again, depending on the complexity and size of your personal organization, you may find that multiple people are following multiple process flows to reach the same end. When this comes to light, it is important to record every step that anyone is doing for your "as-is" process map. It can get messy, but it is the best way to prepare for analyzing your process flow. Once you have created your "as-is" process, it can be documented using software. However, the best reason to do this is for presentation purposes. In a traditional Six Sigma project, you will usually be required to create the "as-is" process using software. In many programs, the Six Sigma Black Belt may do this for you. Working as your own Six Sigma Champion, if you don't have time and don't need to present the information officially to anyone, I suggest simply using the flip chart pages moving forward. Based on your workload and whether or not you need to present the information, this is an example of your being in a position to make the best decision as to whether trying to move your "as-is" process map (which may be messy) to a software program is value-added.

Analyzing Process Flow to Create a "to-Be" Process Map

Process analysis is conducted for the following reasons:

- Assessing the "as-is" process for effectiveness and efficiency
- Identifying underlying causes of any performance inadequacy
- Identifying opportunities for improvement
- Making improvements

Once you've created an "as-is" process flowchart, you and your staff can begin to evaluate the process, looking for redundancies and unnecessary hand-offs, steps, or decisions. You can also evaluate steps that may be creating backlogs, rework, delays, and so on. At the functional level, this discussion can be held at staff meetings or at a one-on-one meeting with the responsible person. In Chapter 2, this activity was classified as both a Process Focus and a Customer Focus and Collaboration activity because your staff is critical to helping identify gaps in the process being that they are closer to the process. To conduct a thorough process analysis, you should utilize activities that fall under the concepts of customer focus and collaboration (Chapter 6) and data driven management (Chapter 7). However, the most obvious place to take a first look is your "as-is" process map. By taking a detailed look at the "as-is" process, managers can search for the following inefficiencies:

- Redundancies—If there is a redundant step, what value is it adding to the process?
- Unnecessary steps or hand-offs—Each hand-off should be scrutinized to determine if it is value-added.
- Decisions—What purpose does each decision serve? Is that purpose critical to the business?
- Backlogs—Is there a bottleneck step?
- Delays—Time frames should be discussed at this point in a general sense to determine where the team suspects there may be delays. This can then be measured, if necessary. Consider that delays are often caused by "desk time" or "shelf time." This means that the product or elements thereof are sitting somewhere waiting for the next process step to take place.

This general process flow analysis is the first step to creating the "to-be" process map. In general, you can improve the overall efficiency of a process by eliminating as many steps, decisions, and hand-offs as possible. Figuring out how best to do this often calls for creative thinking and innovation. It may cause you to examine your personal organizational structure and the job responsibilities of your staff more closely. Examining your "as-is" process will help you identify variables that can be measured to analyze the process via data (see Chapter 7). Once you have performed a complete analysis, you will be ready to create a "to-be" process map. Again, this can be as simple or as complicated as you have time to devote to the exercise. However, a critical step will be to document your improved process. If you prefer to create the "to-be" process using the Sticky Note Method or simply with pencil and paper, it is critical that all aspects of the process are thoroughly documented. This will serve as the basis for piloting the process and then documenting it in a Standard Operating Procedure (SOP). Depending on the number of staff involved in carrying out the process, you may want to document the process in draft form in order to perform a successful pilot. If more than one individual is carrying out the process, they must share a common understanding of the process changes and associated tasks. In this case, if possible, you should transfer the "to-be" process to software.

Another alternative is to write the process out in words and create a high-level process flow with five to seven steps.

Focusing on Process by Piloting New or Changed Processes

DMAIC Stage	Process Activity	Deliverable(s)
Improve	Pilot process change(s)	Updated process maps Pilot run information/learning

When possible, any process change should be piloted prior to full implementation. This is critical to ensure that all bases have been covered and the process will work as envisioned. Piloting a process on a smaller scale allows for details to be ironed out, technological solutions to be tested, and the overall process to be validated. For more minor processes or for smaller scope projects, pilots can often be conducted informally and quickly. Managers should use their "to-be" process documentation to ensure that all involved understand the parameters of the pilot. In addition to "testing" out the process to ensure that all loose strings are tied, data can be collected to compare the "to-be" process to the "as-is" process (see Chapter 7). When possible, any process changes in which I am involved are piloted prior to official implementation. Managers often learn the hard way that full process implementation without testing can lead to some large errors. Some of the unwanted outcomes of skipping the pilot phase are:

- Learning during training that a minor but critical process step has been left out.
- Learning during implementation that the process documentation is confusing and therefore causing human error or confusion.
- Forgetting factors during planning stages that may cause major errors to occur during implementation.

Depending on your particular job or industry, these situations can have various impact levels; however, these can all be avoided by proper piloting of processes. Some of the best scenarios in which managers can pilot new processes within their own scope of work are running the process for:

- A limited time frame
- A select product or customer
- A limited scope such as only a portion of the staff, machines, etc.

When conducting a pilot you will learn what works, what doesn't, and what changes or modifications could improve the new process. The data collected and lessons learned should be documented so that they can be used to update the process map. Once managers have documented lessons learned from the pilot, the final process can be fully documented in the form of an SOP.

Focus on Process by Institutionalizing Improvements

DMAIC Stage	Process Activity	Deliverable(s)
Control	Institutionalize improvement	Process checklists and forms Effective Standard Operating Procedure (SOP)

Once you have determined the new process flow, it is critical to document the process in an SOP or a Standard Working Practice (SWP) (also sometimes called "Job Aids"). Most highly regulated industries are required to have SOPs; however, even if a regulatory agency doesn't require them, they are valuable tools for any organization. These are the terms used for process documentation in many industries, particularly those that are highly regulated, such as the pharmaceutical industry. For nonregulated industries, in reality, it doesn't matter what you call the documents. The key is documenting your process to ensure that there is a common understanding of that process. Explaining the process in more detail or in a more narrative form goes a long way toward ensuring ongoing process consistency for your personal organization. It is extremely useful for training new staff. Long-standing staff can periodically refer to it or use it day to day, depending on the complexity of your processes. It's amazing how quickly a process can branch out and grow when steps are not taken to ensure consistency.

Along with developing flowcharts and process documentation, Process Checklists are essential for many processes. Process Checklists ensure that all steps have been completed. Depending on the process, checklists may or may not be appropriate. They are particularly helpful for redundant processes including many steps completed by one person. Process Checklists are also useful for manual work-flow processes where paperwork is handed off to many individuals. Checklists should be easy to complete and should include ample space for any information that must be recorded.

SOPs should, at a minimum, include the following three sections:

1. Purpose—What is the purpose of the process? What is the intended outcome and deliverable?
2. Scope—What is the scope of the process? Whom does it apply to? What sites or offices does it apply to?
3. Process steps and responsibilities—This is where each process step is recorded and, with it, the titles of those responsible.

Several other sections that are often helpful are:

- Definitions—This provides a common understanding of the terms used within the process.
- Policies—This may or may not be appropriate but is a section in which concrete policies related to the process can be documented. Some organizations have policy documents. If your company has policy documents, I would not reiterate the policies within a process document, but ensure that your process adheres to policy.
- References—You may want to list related process documents, regulatory references, company policy documents, and so forth to clarify for everyone the documents that have impacted your process design.

It is a great idea to include a high-level process map in your SOP or process document. This also is a judgment call depending on the type of processes for which you are responsible. Even in regulated industries, there is no detailed guidance or regulation that tells how to write an SOP. However, if your company has a guidance or template in place, you should, of course, adhere to it.

When writing SOPs, the following points should be considered:

- The educational level and experience of those responsible for carrying out the process. SOPs should be written so that those performing the process can clearly understand the process steps. If you have a mix of education levels and backgrounds, you should always write to the lowest level.
- The native language of those responsible for carrying out the process. Again, if there is a global audience, the language should be as simple as possible while getting the message across.
- Each process step should begin with an action word. Create an action statement. If added explanation is needed, it can be written in paragraph form underneath the action step.
- In regulated industries, you should not document anything that is not critical, as this will leave you open to noncompliance. For example, if the action step is to forward adverse event documents to BRM, do not specify that the documents must be forwarded via fax if it is okay to forward the documents via express mail or other means. Minor things such as using a black pen or stapling pages together should not be included. These are simple examples, but this type of thinking should be applied when considering details to be included in SOPs.

Once you have written the SOP, it is important to control distribution of the document. There are different ways to control documents, and determining the most appropriate will depend on your personal organization, what document control process your company has in place, whether you are in a regulated industry, and the size and complexity of your personal organization.

The Bottom Line

- The DMAIC methodology serves to *define* a process to improve, *measure* the baseline and target performance of the process, *analyze* process data to determine the key process inputs that affect outputs, *improve* the process to optimize outputs, and, finally, *control* the improved process. Middle managers can apply the same methodology and focus on process to improve the efficiency and effectiveness of their personal organizations.

- Understanding the process-related activities and deliverables and why these are important for any scope of work will help you achieve the goal of implementing Six Sigma.

- Being clear on the boundaries in which you have to work is particularly important if you are interested in implementing Six Sigma in a company that does not have a traditional Six Sigma program in place.

- Creating a SIPOC for your chosen process will help you clarify the process scope as applied to your personal organization and the amount of process changes and activities over which you have influence.

- Defining the outputs and inputs for a process leads to identifying metrics for managing the process. In addition, identifying and ensuring a mutual understanding of the inputs and outputs leads to proper identification of suppliers and customers.

- This general Process Flow Analysis is the first step toward creating the "to-be" process map. In general, you can improve the overall efficiency of a process by eliminating as many steps, decisions, and hand-offs as possible. Figuring out how best to do this often calls for creative thinking and innovation. It may cause you to examine more closely your personal organizational structure and the job responsibilities of your staff.

- When possible, any process change should be piloted prior to full implementation. This is critical to ensure that all bases have been covered and the process will work as envisioned.

- Most highly regulated industries are required to have SOPs; however, even if a regulatory agency doesn't require them, they are valuable tools for any organization. The key is documenting your process to ensure that there is a common understanding of that process.

Chapter 6

Customer Focus and Collaboration

You can close more business in two months by becoming interested in other people than you can in two years by trying to get people interested in you.

—Dale Carnegie

No matter how wonderful you and your staff think your product or service is, it will fall flat if it fails to address the desires and needs of your customers. Eventually your customers will go elsewhere or, at the very least, stop expecting to get what they want from you. In the case of internal customers, they may become resentful, more difficult to work with, or worse, complain to senior management. These negative scenarios are some of the more extreme customer actions. Dissatisfied internal customers can consciously or subconsciously create delays and inefficiencies in the workplace. You may notice that individuals slowly or suddenly:

- Become harder to reach via phone
- Don't return e-mails promptly
- Stop copying you on important emails
- Place less priority on review or approvals you require
- Delay meeting with you or your team

Depending on your line of work, this can potentially result in major issues for you and your staff, including missed deadlines. Customer relationship building, whether external or internal, is critical because while we all have heard that "the customer is always right," sometimes they're wrong. There must be avenues to address those situations, scenarios, or moments while maintaining strong positive relationships.

In our competitive world, including the marketplace and workplace, all organizations, and most people, aspire to have a competitive advantage. On a personal level, the competitive advantage you seek may revolve around pleasing senior management, building a strong reputation for providing high quality deliverables or services, or being respected in your field for your particular expertise. Regardless, over time, the opinions of your internal suppliers and customers (including your staff and supervisor) play a key role in meeting these personal goals.

A key Six Sigma concept is customer focus and closely tied to it is another—collaboration. These together make for powerful cornerstone concepts that can strengthen your management framework, creating the underlying energy to support your focus on process and goal of managing your business using data. So how do you know that your product or service truly meets external or internal customer needs? You could just ask. That's the simplest approach, and it can work beautifully for the most basic customer situations. However, depending on your industry and specific responsibilities, asking customers what they need and desire can get complicated. You may have multiple customers that need to be satisfied with the same deliverable. You may have multiple deliverables, each with a different customer.

There are numerous Six Sigma activities that call for customer focus and collaboration. However, collaboration should begin on day one—whether it is day one of your job, the first day you meet the customer, or the day after you finish this book. To build a framework, managers and their staff must practice the principles of collaboration daily. As you plant seeds through small acts of collaboration, you will strengthen the possibility for phenomenal collaboration when it's needed. Collaborate on small issues and when you need critical collaboration, or even strong buy-in from suppliers or customers to achieve a major goal, they will be there, ready and willing to discuss and negotiate.

Once you're ready to tackle a process improvement project using the DMAIC cycle, your ability to collaborate with both your suppliers and customers will increase if you've laid the groundwork by taking the time and initiative to build those relationships. For this reason, a common understanding of the organizational deliverables, suppliers, and customers should be established even before you set out to improve processes. Defining the key outputs or deliverables, core processes, suppliers and customers for your personal organization should be established up front—outside the scope of the DMAIC cycle—to begin building your personal framework. However, once you've selected a specific process to improve, interaction with suppliers and customers will take on a heightened focus as you move through the DMAIC cycle. Table 6.1 shows some of the most straightforward, value-added DMAIC activities that call for customer focus and collaboration, and the resulting deliverables.

Table 6.1 Customer Focused and Collaborative Activities within the DMAIC Model

DMAIC Stage	Customer Focused and Collaborative Activity	Deliverable(s)
Define	Identify suppliers and customers Identify stakeholders Conduct Voice of the Customer (VOC) exercise Create Kano Analysis	Final SIPOC Kano Model
Measure	Identify Critical to Quality (CTQ) items, steps, etc. Create Operational Definitions	Prioritized CTQ List Prioritized Customer Needs List Operational Definitions
Analyze	Create Cause and Effect (Fishbone) Diagram Determine value of process steps	Cause and Effect Analysis Value Analysis
Improve	Brainstorm about solutions Evaluate impact versus effort Create communication plan Create training plan	Tree Diagram for Solutions Impact/Effort Matrix Communication Plan Training Plan
Control	Share successes with stakeholders	Communicated project success

Customer Focus and Collaborating during the Define Stage

DMAIC Stage	Customer Focused and Collaborative Activity	Deliverable(s)
Define	Identify suppliers and customers Identify stakeholders Conduct Voice of the Customer (VOC) exercise Create Kano Analysis	Final SIPOC Kano Model

Identification of Supplier, Customers, and Stakeholders

Before you can understand what your customers need and want, before you can understand how to work better with your suppliers, and before you can understand the concerns of any additional stakeholders, you must know who they are. Who are they *exactly*? For example, in the pharmaceutical industry, many people automatically say that our customers are patients, while others say our primary customer is the FDA and other global regulatory agencies. Regulatory agencies expect us to satisfy them so that they can ensure that patients are safe. While I agree that these are key customers of the pharmaceutical industry, on a functional level we can delve down into the details of our day-to-day work and find numerous internal and external customers on which to focus. Focusing on these more personal suppliers, customers, and stakeholders will improve the quality of our day-to-day work. Improving the quality of the day-to-day work, day in and day out, project by project, and issue by issue, paves the way toward personally impacting each patient and satisfying regulatory agencies. This is how we can best keep our patients safe. And this is where we can find the energy to make that more personal impact we all crave.

Managers and their staffs should have a clear, shared understanding of who the suppliers and customers are. Suppliers and customers are stakeholders, but there will be others. Anyone who has a vested interest in your deliverable is a stakeholder. This includes your supervisor. Depending on your specific responsibilities, only you and your staff will be able to identify all the stakeholders. These individuals or groups usually make up the distribution list for communicating project progress. In many situations, the stakeholders can be makers or breakers since their support is important for your success.

When trying to identify key deliverables, processes, suppliers, and customers outside the DMAIC cycle, the best approach is to fully engage your staff. Create the SIPOCs together. Even if it's just you and one person, sit down together and discuss these characteristics of his or her day-to-day work. Again, this is a key step in moving your personal organization into your new framework.

Johnson & Johnson Example

Using the example of processing and evaluating individual adverse event cases described in Chapter 5, suppliers and customers have been added to the SIPOC shown in Table 6.2.

An exercise to identify key customers resulted in identification of two categories. The two categories and the customers that fall within these two categories, as well as a brief explanation are provided here. I have also indicated whether the customer is internal or external to BRM.

1. Customers who retrieve the completed regulatory form from the BRM database for the purpose of regulatory reporting. Falling into this category are:
   - Ex-U.S. Market Authorization Holders (MAHs)—external
   - U.S.-based MAHs including:
     - J&J Pharmaceutical Research & Development (PRD)—external
     - Centocor, Inc.—external
   - BRM Submissions Group—internal
2. Customers who rely on listings of the processed adverse event data to analyze aggregate data and compile aggregate reports required by regulatory

Table 6.2 J&J BRM Example SIPOC

Process:	Processing and evaluating of individual adverse event cases
Start Boundary:	Adverse event case is received by BRM
End Boundary:	Adverse event case is "promoted" in the computer system for worldwide distribution

Supplier(s)	Input(s)	PROCESS	Output(s)	Customer(s)
Ex-U.S. Market Authorization Holders and their licensing partners (MAHs)	Adverse event source documentation (raw data)	Receive and sort adverse event cases	Processed data Regulatory forms	Ex-U.S. Market Authorization Holders (MAHs)
		Register cases into computer system		U.S.-based MAHs
U.S.-based MAHs and their licensing partners		Process case data through system		BRM Submissions Group
		Manually code adverse events		BRM Aggregate Reports and Analysis Group
		Determine whether the adverse event is expected or not based on approved labeling		BRM Safety Surveillance Group
		Perform medical review of the case		BRM Medical Group
		Perform quality control review		J&J Manufacturing Product Quality

agencies worldwide and/or identify safety trends and signals. Falling into this category are:

- BRM Aggregate Reports and Analysis Group—internal
- BRM Safety Surveillance Group—internal
- BRM Medical Group—internal
- J&J Manufacturing Product Quality—external

You will notice that the suppliers of our adverse event source data are also our customers. This is a good example of a situation in which customer focus and collaboration can be doubly impacted through development of positive relationships.

Understanding the Voice of the Customer (VOC)

Customers are a top priority in Six Sigma. They serve as the starting and ending points for determining success. The customer's voice should be heard. No matter how many degrees, years of experience, or creative ideas you may have, if you don't meet the needs of your customers, you're somehow missing the point. You can continue to guess, or assume you know what your external or internal customers want and need, but this may be an exercise in futility. Despite any communication, personal, or global challenges you may be faced with, finding out what customers want directly from them is the key to getting it right in the end.

What "Voice of the Customer Analysis" boils down to for the functional manager is asking your customers what they want and need from your personal organization. In many cases, managers believe they already know the answers to these critical questions, particularly for the most straightforward processes and deliverables. This may be because the manager's responsibilities have been passed down through organization changes, a promotion, or by joining an organization at the management level. There is often a learning curve associated with new responsibilities or an increase in scope. In general, it takes six months to a year for a new manager to become established in an organization, depending on his or her level of experience and how closely related past experiences are to the new responsibilities. The opposite scenario also exists—there are managers who have been around for years, diligently managing the same processes. They don't see a compelling reason to question the process or their customers. In this case, having the "If it ain't broke, don't fix it" mentality may be preventing process improvement. Finding out what your customers want and need may be as simple as scheduling a meeting and asking them directly. When possible, the best option is to sit face to face with your customers. For organizations that have many customers, group meetings to obtain feedback and surveys are useful options.

Once you've properly defined your deliverables and customers, the next step is to take a look at any available information you have on customer needs, complaints, comments, surveys, etc. The main point is that you shouldn't guess. If there is no available data, you will certainly need to collect some either via face-to-face discussions or a survey. When dealing primarily with internal customers, you must, of course, always consider the end customer as well. Use common sense when discussing feasibility with internal customers. If they would love to have an end of the month deadline to review your report, but the final report is due to the client at the end of the month, it's not going to work. This is an example of a situation where brainstorming with your customer may lead to some interesting ideas, and perhaps a joint effort to impact a larger piece of the process. Once you have compiled data directly from the customer, the next step is to translate customer needs into observable, measurable requirements. This is an important step toward managing your processes and success by using metrics. Once you have written customer requirements, it is important to validate them by showing them to the customer(s). With their feedback, requirements can be refined and finalized. Depending on the scope of your personal organization and how many customers you have, there is a reasonable range of how much time and effort are required to complete an accurate set of customer requirements. However, when dealing with your own internal processes and deliverables, senior management approval or support should not be a limiting factor for accomplishing this task.

Performing a Kano Analysis

Dr. Noriaki Kano was a strong contributor to the Japanese quality movement. He realized the advantages of dividing customers' requirements into three categories:

1. *Basic Requirements.* These are basic requirements that, if missing, will make your customers extremely unhappy. When they are there, the customer won't particularly notice since they are expected. For example, did you even produce the report that is required?

2. *Variable Requirements.* These are the requirements that will either cause your customers to rate your deliverables high or low. For example, how satisfied is the customer with the report content? Did you provide the report on time? Does it include all the appropriate sections?

3. *Latent Requirements.* These are features that go beyond what the customer even imagined. It includes features that the customer may not have been able to express because they are highly innovative or creative. These types of features may result from your staff's going the extra mile. They are often referred to as *customer delighters*. For example, perhaps the report is provided early,

with a colored cover or an index. The trick to delighting internal customers, though, is to make sure that they care about the "extras" you're providing. These types of features should never be provided at the expense of meeting basic or variable requirements. Don't consistently submit your paper late because it takes too long to create the index!

Performing a Kano Analysis is basically categorizing the customer requirements so that you can determine the feasibility of meeting each one. Also it is key to remember that customer requirements may change over time, so ongoing customer relations and validation of requirements are needed to maintain a strong level of customer satisfaction. At first, having an index at the end of each report may have been a latent requirement, but it may evolve into a basic customer requirement. What delighted your internal customers six months ago may now be expected. If you don't keep it up, they may feel that your quality or service is slipping. Continually understanding customer requirements and finding ways to delight them is an aspect of continuous improvement.

Customer Focus and Collaboration during the Measure Stage

DMAIC Stage	Customer Focused and Collaborative Activity	Deliverable(s)
Measure	Identify Critical to Quality (CTQ) items, steps, etc. Create Operational Definitions	Prioritized CTQ List Prioritized Customer Needs List Operational Definitions

Determining What Is Critical to Quality

In general, managers may need to make a judgment call as to which requirements their organization will measure based on the Kano Analysis and the goals and objectives passed down from senior management.

When working within your own scope of work, it may not be feasible to measure every customer requirement, given your resources. Therefore, focusing efforts on the process you've identified for improvement will help narrow the scope of your measurement activities. Once armed with a solid set of customer requirements as defined above, you can define measurements for customer requirements specifically related to the process you've chosen to improve via the DMAIC cycle.

A Critical to Quality (CTQ) Tree can be created to express the relationship between measurements and customer requirements. It is a valuable activity that provides a common understanding of what is going to be measured and why. It is a relatively simple activity that you can work on with your staff, allowing for collaboration and team building. Here's how it works:

Creating a CTQ Tree

1. Identify an output that is important to customers based on your SIPOC, customer requirements list, and Kano Analysis.
2. Identify a characteristic of that output that is "critical to quality" also based on your customer requirement list and Kano Analysis. Write this in a box on the left-hand side of a piece of flipchart paper.
3. Brainstorm with your staff to identify specific kinds of data associated with the Critical to Quality characteristic. Using basic logic, write the ideas for data in boxes moving to the left. As you move to the left, try to boil down the data more specifically. For example, if the deliverable is a report, you many have two boxes to the left of the report: timeliness and document quality. Moving to the left, you would then break down timeliness and document quality. What are the time-related requirements? What are some categories of quality that can be measured? Here are a few:
   - Accuracy of text to tables within the text
   - Accuracy of in-text tables to data provided in appendices
   - Inclusion of confusing statements
   - Grammar

In the end, you should have measurable metrics such as "number of text to table discrepancies per page" or "number of confusing statements per document." Depending on the type of work you do and your outputs, these lists will be very different. The main point is to link measures to your outputs based on customer requirements. For small organizations, this exercise may be as simple as sitting with your direct reports to discuss how you can link customer requirements to measurements for the key deliverable.

Creating Operational Definitions

Once you and your staff have determined what should be measured and have validated the measurements with the customer(s), the next step is to create Operational Definitions. This merely involves defining the measurements in sentence form to provide a shared understanding of what is being measured. If you ultimately create a Metric Dashboard (see Chapter 7), you will most likely have to abbreviate your metrics. If you share the Dashboard with others, they will most likely have to guess as to what you are actually measuring. Therefore, it's important to collaborate with your staff to develop definitions for your metrics. Again, to ensure that everyone is in agreement, share the definitions with the customer(s). Each time metrics are distributed, they should be accompanied by Operational Definitions.

Customer Focus and Collaboration during the Analyze Stage

DMAIC Stage	Customer Focused and Collaborative Activity	Deliverable(s)
Analyze	Create Cause and Effect (Fishbone) Diagram Determine whether process steps are value-added	Cause and Effect Analysis Value Analysis

Exploring Cause and Effect

It's a good idea to put some structure around brainstorming about possible causes of problems within the process you've chosen to improve. Collaborating with your staff, and even customers, to perform a Cause and Effect Analysis is very simple and doesn't have to take too much time. This exercise can help identify major cause(s) of the problem, identify potential root causes, and determine potential solutions. It addition, it can lay the groundwork for planning and implementing a process change or solution.

Here's how it works:

1. Write the problem at the head of a Fishbone Diagram.
2. Identify appropriate cause categories through brainstorming. Write these at the end of each arm of the fishbone.
3. Brainstorm potential causes for each category, keeping in mind how individual causes may impact more than one cause category.
4. Determine the relationship between individual causes in each category.
5. Use data gathered, voting, or consensus to select most likely or important causes that need further investigation.

When performing this exercise with your staff, the value of constructing the Fishbone Diagram is to show visually that everyone has been heard, that you've worked as a team to identify causes for the problem under discussion, and that you've documented your brainstorming session in a way that is constructive. Even if you construct a Fishbone Diagram sitting across from one person who is responsible for the process under discussion, it's a valuable way to dive down into the process and surrounding factors to find root causes. Many people tend to focus on the larger categories rather than pushing deeper into their understanding of the work they do day to day.

If the team gets stumped when trying to force detailed causes into broader categories, affinity diagramming can be very useful as it can allow you to tackle cause and effect from the other end. Begin with identifying the detailed causes and then group them into broader categories. Once you've identified the categories, you can construct the Fishbone Diagram. Then look at the diagram as a team and discuss what you see. Certainly some root causes and actionable problems will leap out at you. Someone may have identified an issue that no one else considered.

Analyzing Process Value

When evaluating a process or making a process decision, the manager should always consider whether a step or action is value-added for the customer. In a regulatory environment, this should also be a *regulatory risk versus value* discussion. If a large chunk of organizational time is spent on an activity that adds little value and is a low regulatory risk, perhaps time is better spent elsewhere. Once you have a great understanding of customer requirements, you should be able to better understand the value not only of your process output but also of the process itself. With your staff, examine your "as-is" process with value for the customer in mind. Categorize each step as value-added or non-value-added. As you move toward creating the "to-be" process, plan to focus on any non-value-added steps. These will be steps that you can move, improve by reducing time, combine with other steps, or cut out altogether. It is important to involve your staff in this activity so that they will understand why the process is going to change. They will be more accepting of change if they have played a key role in creating the change. They will feel more connected to the process and will share the satisfaction of knowing that they have improved the day-to-day workflow that they carry out.

Customer Focus and Collaboration during the Improve Stage

DMAIC Stage	Customer Focused and Collaborative Activity	Deliverable(s)
Improve	Brainstorm about solutions Evaluate impact versus effort Create communication plan Create training plan	Tree Diagram for Solutions Impact/Effort Matrix Communication Plan Training Plan

Analyzing Impact versus Effort

Once you've brainstormed to create a list of new ideas or options for solutions that address the root causes of your process problem, as noted in Chapter 2, it's helpful

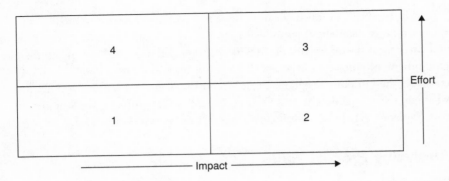

Figure 6.1   An Impact/Effort Matrix.

to evaluate impact versus effort to decide which process improvement options to implement. Every solution may not be practical. The effort required might not be worth the impact that it will have on the process. It may require financial resources that are just not there. Creating an Impact/Effort Matrix is helpful when facing competing actions or solutions. Armed with the list of solutions, you and your staff can discuss each in terms of impact and effort. The impact and effort levels involved can be rated on a scale of one to four. The group should discuss such questions as:

For Impact:

- Will our customer notice this benefit? Immediately? In the long term?
- Will choosing this option bring noticeable relief to those working downstream in the process?
- Does the solution impact the biggest issues for the process?

For Effort:

- Is this solution or change easy to implement?
- What are the resource implications?
- Do we have the technology in place to implement this solution?

Once ratings are given to each solution or option, they can be evaluated by using Figure 6.1.

Communicating Change

Communicating change is a critical factor in managing changes within your personal organization. Communication in stable times impacts culture tremendously, so you can imagine how important it is when processes are changing. Of course, the more you've involved your staff in identifying issues and solutions, the less apprehensive they will be when the change is implemented. However, whether informal or formal, a Communication Plan should be developed to notify and educate all stakeholders regarding coming changes. The Communication Plan can also include a plan for training staff; however, depending on the size of your personal organization and the scope of the change, you may need both a Communication Plan and a Training Plan.

This is an area where the manager must use judgment as to how formal the plan needs to be. Whether or not you work in a regulated industry will also impact the level of documentation surrounding your plan, particularly for training. The main point when implementing Six Sigma within your personal organization is that you should not ignore the importance of carefully planned communications surrounding change. Equally important is providing any training that is needed to effectively implement the new process. In addition to communicating with and training your staff, be careful not to forget other key stakeholders such as your suppliers, customers, and supervisor. If you've maintained a customer focus and a collaborative spirit throughout the DMAIC cycle, your suppliers and customers should be highly supportive of the coming changes. Sometimes developing a Communication Plan is merely planning the key times that you will send out announcements to staff and customers regarding progress and successes.

Customer Focus and Collaboration during the Control Stage

DMAIC Stage	Customer Focused and Collaborative Activity	Deliverable(s)
Control	Share successes with stakeholders	Communicated project success

Understanding the Importance of Ongoing Communication

Once you implement the improved process, you should not be shy about tooting your own horn. Process improvement is a great accomplishment that should be celebrated and shared with others. Announcing your success is an important way that you can show your broader organization that Six Sigma works and that you can follow the DMAIC cycle in your own scope of work. This is also the time to publicly thank internal suppliers and customers with whom you've collaborated to make the change happen.

Regardless of the scope of your work, if the process changes you've identified have created a more satisfied internal or external customer, you've succeeded. In addition, if you've followed the objectives of Six Sigma, you should also be seeing a more efficient process and one that saves resources, including employee time. We all know time is money. Therefore, to some degree, you've impacted the bottom line for your company. Don't be afraid to let everyone know. Success is contagious!

The Bottom Line

- No matter how wonderful you and your staff think your product or service is, it will fall flat if it fails to address the desires and needs of your customers. Dissatisfied internal customers can consciously or subconsciously create delays and inefficiencies in the workplace.

- Customer focus and collaboration make for powerful cornerstone concepts that can strengthen your management framework, creating the underlying energy to support your focus on the process and goal of managing your business using data.

- When trying to identify key deliverables, processes, suppliers, and customers outside the DMAIC cycle, the best approach is to fully engage your staff.

- What "Voice of the Customer Analysis" boils down to for the functional manager is asking your customers what they want and need from your personal organization.

- Depending on the scope of your personal organization and how many customers you have, there is a reasonable range as to how much time and effort are required to complete an accurate set of customer requirements. However, when dealing with your own internal processes and deliverables, senior management approval or support should not be a limiting factor for accomplishing this task.

- Performing a Kano Analysis is basically categorizing the customer requirements so that you can determine the feasibility of meeting each one.

- Once armed with a solid set of customer requirements, you can define measurements for customer requirements specifically related to the process you've chosen to improve via the DMAIC cycle.

- A Critical to Quality (CTQ) Tree can be created to express the relationship between measurements and customer requirements. It is a valuable activity that provides a common understanding of what is going to be measured and why.

Chapter 7

Using Data to Manage within Your Scope

Drive thy business; let it not drive thee.

—Benjamin Franklin

anaging work based on facts and data makes sense. Rounding out the basic Six Sigma concepts of process focus, customer focus, and collaboration, managing by data solidifies an approach that can be applied to your scope of work. The key is identifying the type of data needed according to your unique responsibilities and goals. When you set out to manage by using data, it must be practical. There must be a balance between the effort involved and the value that is added to your personal organization. In the Johnson & Johnson Process Excellence program, data is the final determinant of process excellence. When striving to achieve business excellence, data is still the final determinant, but collecting and analyzing the data must be worth the effort for each process and deliverable under consideration. In your own scope of work, you must pick and choose which processes are critical to success, which steps are critical to quality, and which processes, steps, or deliverables should have associated data. Most likely, you won't have the time or resources needed to evaluate everything using data. And that's okay! Six Sigma was never intended to be an academic exercise; it is intended to bring results to your company, your personal organization, and to you. We must do what it makes sense to do and nothing more. There is certainly a place for gut feelings, intuition, and decision making based on experience in our day-to-day world; however, facts are irrefutable. Managers should evaluate their own business situations to determine where facts are critical for moving the business forward; seeking buy-in from suppliers, customers, or higher management; or simply improving processes.

Table 7.1   Data Driven Activities within the DMAIC Model

DMAIC Stage	Data Driven Activity	Deliverable(s)
Define		
Measure	Identify key process measures Identify sampling strategy Collect process data Calculate sigma	Data Collection Plan Data forms and spreadsheets Process sigma
Analyze	Conduct Pareto Analysis Analyze histograms Analyze run charts	Data analysis for "as-is" process
Improve		
Control	Create Metric Scorecard or Dashboard Create process monitoring tools	Process Control Plan Scorecard or Dashboard

Table 7.1 shows some of the most straightforward, value-added DMAIC data-driven activities and the resulting deliverables. The Measure, Analyze, and Control stages are strongly based on data driven activities, whereas process-focused, customer-focused, and collaborative activities drive the Define and Improve stages. For this reason, this chapter focuses on the Measure, Analyze, and Control stages of the DMAIC cycle.

Data Driven Activities during the Measure Stage

DMAIC Stage	Data Driven Activity	Deliverable(s)
Measure	Identify key process measures Identify sampling strategy Collect process data Calculate sigma	Data Collection Plan Data forms and spreadsheets Process sigma

Creating a Data Collection Plan

When focusing on your own scope of work, the most basic data collection plan centers on identifying and measuring quality and compliance for your key deliverables, which are most often internal deliverables. This is particularly true for straightforward internal processes that have clear deliverables with clear time frames. Timeliness is the easier of the two to measure. Quality metrics are a bit more challenging to define and measure, but can prove extremely valuable over time. Quality and compliance data will serve as control data for a process that's been improved; however, depending on the complexity of your processes, it may make sense to begin evaluating the quality and compliance of your "as-is" process even if you're thinking that it doesn't need improvement. But the point of Six Sigma is process improvement, and the point of business excellence is improving business all around. With this in mind, you've come full circle to the bottom line in Six Sigma. Identify your key processes, measure them, analyze the measurements, improve the processes, and then keep them under control. All this means is that if you have a very straightforward process, you can still measure, analyze, and improve it. It doesn't have to be complicated.

A good Data Collection Plan consists of the following:

- What you are going to measure and the data sources
- Operational Definitions as described in Chapter 6
- Data collection process
- Sampling plan
- Data Collection Forms or spreadsheets
- Explanation of how you intend to analyze the data collected

Remembering that you may or may not have specific support for this work within your personal organization, creating a Data Collection Plan should be reduced to simple steps and documentation. The critical nature of documenting the plan grows with the number of people involved and whether or not you want or need to present the information formally. It's up to you; the bottom line is that you and the others involved understand what is happening and why.

For highly complicated processes or processes involving numerous individuals, once you've identified the key factors via SIPOC creation, the customer requirements, and what's critical to quality and have created Operational Definitions for the data that should be collected, you're ready to create and document a Data Collection Plan that can be followed by assigned staff.

If you have defined your "as-is" process well, you should have a clear understanding of *why* you are measuring *what* you are measuring. Understanding why sounds basic, but it implies that you have an understanding of what is critical to making the process successful and how you can evaluate via data whether success is occurring or not. In most cases, you will want to keep the focus on process efficiency and/or effectiveness. These are things that you and your staff should have identified via process-focused, customer-focused, and collaborative activities. There are two types of data that you may need to collect: continuous and discrete. Things that can be measured on a scale such as time, height, temperature, and money are examples of continuous data. Discrete data is information that can be categorized, such as types of cars, types of food, or levels of satisfaction. These are the measures that often use a five-point scale. As an example, submission dates can be measured on a continuous scale (i.e., submitted on day 5, 10, or 15) or they can be measured discretely as on time versus late (a category). Six

Sigma performance is based on discrete data, the standard being a "defect." When working within your scope, discrete measurements are often the best choice because it's easier and faster to collect discrete data than it is to collect continuous data. Continuous data allows for more precision, but will take more time and resources, which is often impractical. Remember, when implementing your own Six Sigma program, you will need to keep things as simple as possible while accomplishing the goal.

Data Collection Forms are used to collect and organize data. They can also serve as checklists to ensure that all details of the unit (whatever you are focusing on) are reviewed, measured, counted, etc. Data Collection Forms should capture the appropriate data and be easy to use. Spreadsheets can be created and used to compile data collected on the individual Data Collection Forms. The easiest software to use that is routinely available now is Microsoft Excel, although there are other, more sophisticated software packages available. Keep forms to a minimum. Every form you create implies additional process steps such as hand-offs, approvals, filing, etc. I recommend that, when possible, data be recorded the first time electronically via an electronic form or spreadsheet. This makes it easier to analyze the data electronically and is more efficient. In other words, when possible, you should avoid having someone hand record data and then have to enter it into a spreadsheet later to enable analysis. However, depending on what you are measuring, it may be necessary to create hard copy forms for data collection.

Johnson & Johnson Example

Table 7.2 shows an example of how customer requirements were linked to specific business metrics. Some of the metrics displayed in the table were not chosen as critical to quality and, therefore, were not measured. Others were deemed important, but it was determined that the more practical approach would be to verify compliance via routine internal auditing. Following are the customer category definitions:

- Category One. Customers who retrieve the completed regulatory form (MedWatch or CIOMS forms) from the drug safety reporting database for the purpose of regulatory reporting
- Category Two. Customers who rely on listings of the processed adverse event data to analyze aggregate data and compile aggregate reports as required by regulatory agencies worldwide and/or identify safety trends and signals

Note that some of the metrics are applicable for both customer categories.

Table 7.2 Customer Requirements Linked to Specific Business Metrics

Category One	Metric	Category Two	Metric
Accurate duplicate adverse event (AE) report searches to ensure duplicate cases are not created in the database	Number of duplicate cases identified and deleted per month per number of cases processed	Accurate and complete adverse event coding	Number of corrections to AE coding per month by J&J physicians— Also included in quality review of cases against source documents (identifying any events that were not coded)
Acknowledgement of receipt of adverse event source documentation within three business days	Internal Audit	Accurate duplicate searches to ensure duplicates cases are not created	Number of duplicate cases identified and deleted per month/number of cases processed
Accurate and complete adverse event coding	Number of corrections to AE coding per month by Medical Assessment Physicians— Also included in quality review of cases against source documents (identifying any events that were not coded)	Regulatory forms in which narrative data accurately reflects data entered in specific data fields	Quality review— number of errors per case—statistical sample or review in workflow
Completion of serious unexpected associated adverse event summaries for clinical trial cases	Errors per SUA Summary reviewed	Complete and accurate data entry from source documentation provided	Quality review— number of errors per case—statistical sample or review in workflow
On time promotion of serious reports to the Local Reporting Module	Percentage of reports promoted on time (compliance)	Accurate labeling	Include in quality review of cases
On time promotion of serious, life-threatening, death or reports from clinical trials to the Local Case Reporting Module	Percentage of reports promoted on time (compliance)	Completion of processing of all adverse event cases in workflow by the aggregate report data lock	Percentage of cases processed on time (compliance)

(Continues)

Table 7.2   (Continued)

Category One	Metric	Category Two	Metric
Accurate assessment of causality for clinical cases	Internal audit	Adherence to data entry standards so that data is processed consistently	Include in quality review of cases
Regulatory forms in which narrative data accurately reflects data entered in specific data fields	Quality review in workflow—number of errors per case—statistical sample	Prompt notification of product quality issues via the appropriate form	Internal audit
Complete and accurate data entry from source documentation provided	Quality review in workflow—number of errors per case—statistical sample	Notification of signals detected during case processing	Internal audit
Accurate labeling	Internal audit		

Creating a Sampling Strategy

Sampling allows for measurement of a relatively few units compared to measuring every unit. Testing, reviewing, or counting each and every unit in a process can be extremely time consuming and illogical for any organization. The beauty of proper sampling is that you can measure a sample that statistically represents the entire set of data. There are many sampling strategies that can be applied depending on the unique situation, but an easy, general sampling method that works in most functional level scenarios is to define a unit, determine the average number of units for a particular time frame, and then refer to a standard statistical sampling table to determine how many units should be tested, reviewed, or counted to obtain the desired level of confidence that your sample metrics will reflect the entire population. This type of sampling will ensure that your sample is a statistical representation of the entire data set. This is particularly useful when you are trying to understand database quality. We use this method at J&J to determine how many serious adverse event cases should undergo quality assurance review. We consider one case as a unit. Then, to obtain our sample, we determine the average number of cases processed per month over a three-month period. That gives us the total number of units processed per month. Then we use a sampling table to determine our sample (or the number of cases) that we should review each month to ensure that the quality of the sample represents the data quality of all serious adverse event cases processed within the month. We recalculate the sample every three months to ensure that we are still on target, considering that our case volume varies over time. The sampling table that I use is found in B. Scott Parsowith's book, *Fundamentals of Quality Auditing*. However, standard sampling tables can be found in numerous statistics and auditing books.

Other sampling methods can be used to "get a feel for" attributes within a process that have continuously changing variables, which is typical in many businesses. Some examples are:

- Recording the number of adverse events reported per week
- Recording sales volume every half hour
- Tracking the average age of customers by week

When developing metrics for pharmaceutical databases, my aim is to ensure that my results are as statistically significant as I can prove because many people are looking at my results to demonstrate the quality of their work as well as the quality of the processes and standards they must follow.

Calculating Sigma for Your Process

The actual sigma for your process is but one of the many metrics that you can use to understand and monitor product quality. To review from Chapter 1, in statistics, the lowercase Greek letter sigma "σ" is the symbol for standard deviation, which describes the degree of variation in a data set, a group of items, or a process. A six sigma level of quality means that there are fewer than 3.4 defects, or deviations from the standard, per million units produced. It is a technical measure of customer satisfaction.

Calculating sigma for your process is actually not that difficult. First you have to understand what should be considered as a unit in your process. A unit can be an item processed, such as piece of data, or the final product or service being delivered to an internal or external customer, such as a processed adverse event case. A defect is a failure to meet the customer requirements or a performance standard. For an adverse event case, a data entry error can be considered a defect, or a case with at least one error can be considered a defective deliverable. So, basically, the *unit* is the items that you're concerned about and *defects* are errors. Based on your line of work and the types of processes for which you are responsible, you will need to determine what is an appropriate unit and what is considered a defect for that unit.

A unit can be any product or service or your job's deliverables. The principles of Six Sigma can be applied to many different situations. Consider adverse event cases as an example. If, in a sample of 100 cases, 20 *defective cases* (defined as a case with at least one critical error; one must also define *critical* here) were found, that would mean 0.20 or 20 percent defects, or that 80 percent of units were acceptable. According to the sigma conversion table shown here as Table 7.3, this percentage of acceptable units falls between sigma levels of 2 and 3. At a 2 sigma, you

Table 7.3 Six Sigma Conversions

Percent of Acceptable Units	Sigma Level	Defects/Million Units
99.99966	6σ	3.4
99.98	5σ	233
99.4	4σ	6,210
93.3	3σ	66,807
69.1	2σ	308,537
30.9	1σ	690,000

can expect 308,537 defects per 1 million adverse event cases processed and at a 3 sigma you can expect 66,807 defects per 1 million cases. Of course, at J&J we do not processes anything close to 1 million adverse event cases in a given year. However, theoretically, we would not want to make 308,537 case processing errors as this could potentially compromise patient safety over time. Adverse event case data is eventually assessed as aggregate data compiled for specific time frames. We want our data to be as accurate as possible to ensure that our assessment of adverse events is accurate, which therefore allows for accurate assessment of risk versus benefit for our patients.

Six Sigma is about much more than merely calculating and banking on a sigma value. Depending on your business, if calculating the sigma for a process does not add value by hitting close enough to home, don't do it. Instead, focus on using the DMAIC cycle and other value-added metrics to gain process understanding, and to drive decision making. However, one must remember that Six Sigma is based on the goal of having a near perfect process that brings your deliverables to a Six Sigma level of quality according to customer requirements. The beauty of Six Sigma as a business philosophy is that it allows flexibility. Even top companies such as J&J that have implemented Six Sigma throughout their businesses strive to use Six Sigma tools and methodologies in ways that make sense for the business at hand. Some people feel that it's a cookie cutter method, but it's not. You can bring your creativity and business acumen to play when implementing Six Sigma. That's the challenge!

Data Driven Activities during the Analyze Stage

DMAIC Stage	Data Driven Activity	Deliverable(s)
Analyze	Conduct Pareto Analysis Analyze histograms Analyze run charts	Data analysis for "as-is" process

Pareto Analysis

A Pareto chart is an easy way to show the relative importance of causes, defects, and other aspects of your "as-is" process. To review, the chart is based on the rule of thumb coined by Italian economist Vilfredo Pareto. He said that 80 percent of all problems result from 20 percent of the causes (commonly known as the 80/20 rule). For example, if errors are categorized into types, a Pareto chart is merely a visual method of showing how the errors are broken down into those categories and the percentages. Pareto charts are used for discrete data because the chart demonstrates which categories of your data are causing the greatest impact. In other words, what issues make up for the 20 percent that is causing 80 percent of your problems? If you know that, you've already accomplished a great deal toward solving 80 percent of your problems, which is quite significant. In order to create a Pareto chart, you must first categorize your defects. This is why it's best not merely to record data such as defect-yes, defect-no. That will help with your Sigma calculation, but it will not help you determine how best to reduce the total number of defects. For instance, if you are measuring "on time versus late," you should also categorize the reasons for lateness. There are numerous software programs that allow for quick generation of Pareto charts, including Microsoft Excel. Figure 7.1

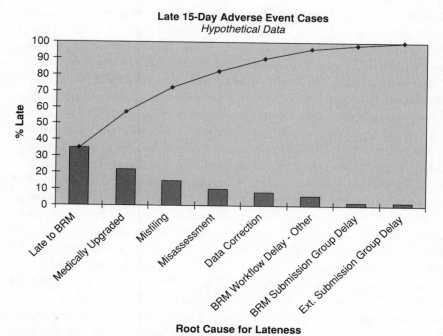

Figure 7.1   Pareto Chart Example

is a *theoretical* example of reasons why applicable adverse event cases were submitted to the FDA beyond the required 15-day time frame:

In my work, at J&J, if we were analyzing this Pareto chart, we would conclude that focusing our efforts on lateness that is caused by late submission of cases to BRM by our operating companies could potentially make a tremendous impact on our timeliness. This is the type of simple data that can build consensus for strategy and for goal setting that will be well worth the efforts contributed by your staff. And as always, if you need to present this data or provide justification for decisions and actions, the Pareto chart is a beautiful visual of your analysis. That sure beats saying, "Well, based on my experience this year, we need to focus our efforts on . . . in order to hit our targets." Of course, sometimes that statement may fly, but sometimes it won't—it's up to you as a manager to determine whether or not the Pareto chart will add value. In most cases, I believe it will.

Understanding Variability by Using Run Charts and Histograms

A *run chart* is merely a running log of continuous data (a measurement) over a specified time frame as shown in Figure 7.2. Basically, process performance is measured over time. The data is usually represented in a line chart. Changes over time can be identified and investigated. How the data points fall across the chart can be compared to a target data points for the particular data being measured. Run charts are also easy to create and interpret, and therefore can add a lot of value with little effort. In order to make an accurate interpretation of the data, you must collect enough data. It is generally recommended that an average of 50 data points be collected. Run charts are also sometimes referred to as time plots or trend plots. It's important when looking for trends over time to understand when you are seeing data change due to a special cause. A special cause is a unique situation that would not normally occur, such as failure of a critical machine during a manufacturing process. When evaluating run charts, the focus should be on common variation. Variation in processes is normal; however, one of the goals of a traditional Six Sigma team is to find ways to decrease common variation so that the variability around your target becomes smaller and smaller. Creating and evaluating a run chart over time will help you determine whether or not the variation in your process is getting larger or smaller. The charted data will not tell you what is causing the variation around the target, but it will help guide you over time as you make changes to the process. For example a run chart could be maintained for BRM compliance to 15-day adverse event submissions to the FDA. If our compliance maintained a fairly tight variation over time, but then fell dramatically during one particular month, we could then assess what happened that month to

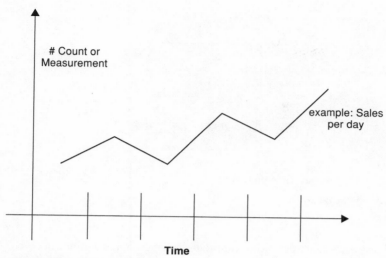

Figure 7.2   Run Chart

determine why the compliance fell. Perhaps we know that during that particular month, one of our regional case processing centers was closed unexpectedly due to an asbestos problem in the building. The staff was forced to leave the premises immediately and could not access the data in order to process it. There may be situations such as this one that cannot be helped; this is an example of "for cause" variation. What we can help and improve is the normal expected variation that impacts the process and resulting outcome. The main focus should be to watch the variation around your specified goal. If the line falls over time so that it is flattening below the goal, for example, it would be prudent to determine what caused the downward shift in the normal variation and correct it.

To look at the data you've collected over time, you can also create a histogram as shown in the Figure 7.3. A histogram is a vertical bar chart where the height of each bar shows the number of data points that are represented in a particular data range. To create a histogram, the data that you've collected over time is divided into fractions. The data is then presented as a bar graph where the vertical axis represents the frequency and the horizontal axis defines the buckets. This shows the distribution of the data you've collected over a specific time frame. Histograms can help you see the pattern and shape of that distribution. The distribution of data can help predict future performance of the process. It also helps to indicate if there has been a change in the process. When evaluating the histogram, some questions that do not require a high degree of statistical knowledge that are helpful for managers are:

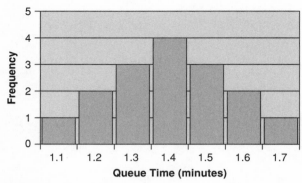

Figure 7.3   Histogram

- Is the process centered? This means that the data should be somewhat evenly distributed around your target. If the bars are all shifted to the left or right of your target, the process is not centered and the process data is running too high or too low.
- What is the shape of the bar graph? Does it follow a bell-shaped curve, which is a normal distribution? Most processes will not follow an exact bell-shaped curve; however, studying the shape can provide an indication of process issues. If there are twin or multiple peaks, this indicates that the data is coming from two different sources (e.g., shifts, machines, people, etc). In this case, the data should be stratified. This means that taking the same buckets of data, you create separate histograms for each data source. They could be people, times of day, etc. This will allow you to begin to link your data to specific situations within your workflow.

Data Driven Activities during the Control Stage

DMAIC Stage	Data Driven Activity	Deliverable(s)
Control	Create Metric Scorecard or Dashboard Create process monitoring tools	Process Control Plan Scorecard or Dashboard

Creating a Process Control Plan

Once you and your direct reports or team have analyzed the data collected for your "as-is" process and have determined how you can best improve that process, the key to maintaining control of your process is to create a Process Control Plan. This can be as simple or as complicated as it needs to be, depending on your particular situation. The run chart is probably the simplest tool that can be used when seeking to maintain control on processes within your scope. The Process Control Plan can be formally documented, or it can be an understanding between you and your direct reports that they will maintain a run chart and provide data to you periodically. You can require a report including ongoing analysis or status. It's up to you. The key is keeping an eye on what you've established as an improved process via the use of data. The plan may entail the creation and distribution of Metrics Dashboards or scorecards. I prefer to call them Dashboards because I feel this is a more positive term. Any organization, regardless of scope, can create metrics for its key deliverables.

Using Metrics Dashboards

A Metrics Dashboard is merely a template for communicating those metrics to the applicable audiences, whether that is just you as the self-empowered manager acting as Six Sigma Champion for your team or if it's your senior management, customers, and/or other stakeholders. Dashboards display the key metrics (data) needed to ensure that the process is delivering as intended. The data provided should enable decision making about the process. The single most important factor for using a Dashboard is to make sure that the data being provided is what is needed. Is it useful?

The scope of your responsibility will dictate how sophisticated your metrics Dashboard(s) should be. A Dashboard is usually a one-page table that lists the metrics being tracked, the metric data for each time frame, and the target metric as shown in the example below. Metrics that are considered risky or unacceptable can be highlighted.

Johnson & Johnson Example

Figure 7.4 represents the Dashboard used by my own organization to communicate single adverse event case quality metrics and the Operation Definitions. The distribution list for Metrics Dashboards should be included in the Process Control Plan. In addition, you can include the process for addressing metrics that fall below acceptable levels. For some situations, you may need to define an escalation process such that issues are addressed within an appropriate time frame. This is not a cookie-cutter approach; it must be applied in a logical and practical way to your particular business processes, goals and objectives, and organizational structure. This is your job!

The Bottom Line

- Rounding out the basic Six Sigma concepts of process focus, customer focus, and collaboration, managing by data solidifies an approach that can

Figure 7.4 Single Case Processing Quality Management Report

Regional Center	Metric Category	Base-line	Feb	Mar	Apr	May	Jun	Jul	Aug	Sep	Oct	Nov	Dec	Year to Date Avg.	Target
2005															
Overall	Mean no. findings per case														
	Mean no. suggestions per case														
	Percent with 0 findings/suggestions														
	Percent with 0 findings														
	Percent with 1 or more findings														
NSA East	Mean no. findings per case														
	Mean no. suggestions per case														
	Percent with 0 findings/suggestions														
	Percent with 0 findings														
	Percent with 1 or more findings														
NSA West	Mean no. findings per case														
	Mean no. suggestions per case														
	Percent with 0 findings/suggestions														
	Percent with 0 findings														
	Percent with 1 or more findings														
UK	Mean no. findings per case														
	Mean no. suggestions per case														
	Percent with 0 findings/suggestions														
	Percent with 0 findings														
	Percent with 1 or more findings														

Operational Definitions

Overall
- Mean no. findings per case — Average number of significant errors/omissions per case
- Mean no. suggestions per case — Average number of minor errors/omissions per case
- Percent with 0 findings/suggestions — Total percent of cases with no errors or omissions
- Percent with 0 findings — Total percent of cases with no significant errors or omissions
- Percent with 1 or more findings — Total percent of cases with one or more significant errors or omissions

NSA East
- Mean no. findings per case
- Mean no. suggestions per case
- Percent with 0 findings/suggestions
- Percent with 0 findings
- Percent with 1 or more findings

Definitions noted above for Case Processing Center located in the United States—East Coast

NSA West
- Mean no. findings per case
- Mean no. suggestions per case
- Percent with 0 findings/suggestions
- Percent with 0 findings
- Percent with 1 or more findings

Definitions noted above for Case Processing Center located in the United States—West Coast

UK
- Mean no. findings per case
- Mean no. suggestions per case
- Percent with 0 findings/suggestions
- Percent with 0 findings
- Percent with 1 or more findings

Definitions noted above for Case Processing Center located in the United Kingdom be applied to your scope of work. The key is identifying the type of data needed according to your unique responsibilities and goals.

- A manager should evaluate his or her own business situation to determine where facts are critical for moving the business forward, seeking buy-in from suppliers, customers, or higher management, or simply improving processes.

- When focusing on your own scope of work, the most basic data collection plan centers on identifying and measuring quality and compliance for your key deliverables, which are most often internal deliverables.

- Being aware that you may or may not have specific support for this work within your personal organization, creating a Data Collection Plan should be reduced to simple steps and documentation.

- There are two types of data that you may need to collect: continuous and discrete. Things that can be measured on a scale such as time, height, temperature, and money are examples of continuous data. Discrete data is information that can be categorized, such as types of cars, types of food, or levels of satisfaction.

- There are many sampling strategies that can be applied depending on the unique situation, but an easy, general sampling method that works in most functional level scenarios is to define a unit, determine the average number of units for a particular time frame, and then refer to a standard statistical sampling table to determine how many units should be tested, reviewed, or counted to obtain the desired level of confidence that your sample metrics will reflect the entire population.

- The actual sigma for your process is but one of the many metrics that you can use to understand and monitor product quality.

- Depending on your business, if calculating the sigma for a process does not add value by hitting close enough to home, don't do it. Instead, focus on using the DMAIC cycle and other value-added metrics to gain process understanding and to drive decision making.

- A Pareto chart is an easy way to show the relative importance of causes, defects, and other aspects of your "as-is" process.

- A run chart is merely a running log of continuous data (a measurement) over a specified time frame. Performance data is measured over time for a process.

- A histogram is a vertical bar chart where the height of each bar shows the number of data points that are represented in a particular data range.

- Once you and your direct reports or team have analyzed the data collected for your "as-is" process and have determined how you can best improve that process, the key to maintaining control of your process is to create a Process Control Plan.

- A Metrics Dashboard is merely a template for communicating those metrics to the applicable audiences, whether that is just you as the self-empowered manager acting as Six Sigma Champion for your team or if it's your senior management, customers, and/or other stakeholders.

Chapter 8

Strategic Planning for Quality: Pulling It All Together Before You Begin

Getting ready is the secret to success.

—Henry Ford

Focusing on processes and customers, collaboration, and data driven management makes good business sense. These are key concepts in quality management and, thus, Six Sigma. Do we really need a special program to convince us that these concepts are simply elements of excellent business practice? Sometimes I wonder how some people go to work each day and manage as if it were a routine, treating process or people issues that arise by using cookie-cutter methods. That's just not very exciting or innovative; it could be boring. Putting out fires at work isn't boring. But it's frustrating, especially when you have the distinct feeling you put the same fire out about six months ago. Working this way, how can we accomplish something big? Something amazing? We may be able to complete the tasks at hand, but will the scope of our tasks ever grow? Will we ever advance beyond routine management and fire fighting? These are questions that you must ask yourself when deciding whether or not it would be beneficial to create your own strategy for business excellence—one based on Six Sigma.

Creating a strategy begins with establishing the framework in which you plan to operate your organization. Putting a management framework down on paper is the easy part. Practicing what you preach is not always easy or simple. Forget about creating a Pareto chart. Just trying to focus throughout the day on a set of standards you've set for yourself and your staff can be daunting, particularly when faced with stress, problem employees, breakdowns, slowdowns, system failures, inspections, and all the other issues managers may see during any given week. How about the pharmaceutical industry when patient safety is at risk, or hospitals where patients are suffering and could be dying? These are extreme examples, but every person in a management position knows he or she is being counted on to produce, to make things work, and to maneuver around all the issues in order to make that happen.

Many managers are not instructed or encouraged to think strategically until they reach a particular level within the organization. Then, in some cases, you're supposed to know how to shift from being a tactical thinker to a strategic thinker. Sometimes these terms aren't defined for the manager; therefore, the shift is an inward kind of thing that somehow must be demonstrated via actions, communications, and who knows what other types of nonverbal communication and political maneuvering. Creating a strategy that starts with a defined management framework within your own personal organization is an excellent training exercise. Not only will it hone your strategic planning and thinking skills, it will also help you achieve results in a consistent, documented, organized fashion that is visible to your staff and your supervisor.

If one were creative and carefully considered the particular working environment, industry, and responsibilities involved, there are probably numerous strategies encompassing the underlying concepts of Six Sigma that could be applied. Over time, I have created a strategy that works for me. I have applied this strategy to various degrees at three different companies, supervising many different types of people. For me, it has proven to be successful. The simple strategy I created has helped me to:

- Build work teams that share a common vision
- Improve the quality of my organizational deliverables (with data to prove it)
- Improve the quality of deliverables for key functions supported by my own organization (also with data to prove it)
- Build a positive culture where individuals feel that they are part of something important

The Przekop Strategy

Following is my strategy to improve the quality of your organizational outputs.

Step	The Przekop Strategy
1	Create a management framework (and stand behind it).
2	Organize your organization for quality (no matter what the size).
3	Follow the DMAIC cycle for your organization (*only* as appropriate).
4	Continuously monitor and improve your organization (maintain the momentum).

Strategic Step 1: Create a Management Framework

As discussed in Chapter 4, the first step to leading a personal organization by using the Six Sigma cornerstone concepts is to create a management framework that will support your efforts. As a reminder, three questions to consider when developing this critical framework are:

1. What operational concepts/values/norms will serve as the day-to-day cornerstones for your organization, thus driving all interactions and decisions?
2. What is your vision for your organization—what would you like it to look like in five years?
3. What management style is important to you as the organizational leader?

Of course, at J&J, my personal organization is compelled to follow the overarching J&J management framework, which is our Credo. I once heard an analogy at a J&J Leadership Conference that compared our Credo to a crystal ball that we must juggle along with all the other rubber balls we hold as we make management decisions. As we juggle and weigh all those factors to make the best decision, there is always one crystal ball in the mix, our Credo. Whatever we do, we must never drop that crystal ball. Dropping a rubber ball can be overcome, but the crystal is irreplaceable. From that kind of commitment, management integrity is born. Bringing this concept into my own personal organization, I have more intimately defined a management framework that is built upon the J&J Credo. I expect those in my personal organization to focus on this framework as we move among our internal customers, stakeholders, and colleagues. It serves as my second crystal ball.

Johnson & Johnson Example

In Table 8.1, you will see the management framework for my organization with a brief explanation of each point. It only serves as an example, but you can see that it includes the cornerstone concepts of Six Sigma as well as the basic concepts of the J&J Credo. I laminated my management framework statement, presented it at one of my monthly staff meetings, and provided each person with a copy to hang in his or her office or cubicle. When anyone new joins my organization, I review this document with them, explaining how important it is to me and to my organization. Depending on the size and complexity of your organization, it may be beneficial to present your framework to your direct reports, obtain their input, and then finalize the framework as a management team prior to rolling it out to the rest of your organization.

Table 8.1   Global Quality Management (GQM)
           Management Framework

Adherence to the J&J Credo values	Each GQM employee will, at all times, adhere to and support the J&J Credo.
Open communication with team focus	The GQM group will function using an open communication style with a strong team focus. We will openly discuss issues and work together as a team to resolve them. We will also support one another to accomplish the overall goals of our organization.
Respect at all levels	Every member of the GQM team is to be respected as an individual with unique talents, goals, and motivations. Members of the GQM will respect our colleagues, suppliers, and customers represented at all organizational levels, acknowledging that they each play a role in meeting organizational goals.
Strong customer focus and collaboration	Each member of the GQM team will demonstrate at all times a strong customer focus. We recognize that while the customer is not always right, we intend to work with our customers toward the best outcome in any given situation, preserving critical relationships and paving the way for future collaboration.
Positive thinking and behaviors	GQM will function as a positive environment; each employee contributes to that culture. While it is recognized that some days are more challenging than others, we will each strive to look at each glass as half full rather than half empty and support one another at times when this may be difficult.
Data driven management when possible	We will strive to manage our business based on data and facts.
Continuous improvement, both individually and as a team	Each GQM employee will strive to continuously improve his or her knowledge and skill set. As a team, we will strive to continuously improve our organization. We will move toward the future with a shared vision of making a positive and lasting contribution to the larger organization.
Documentation of key monthly deliverables	Monthly deliverables will be established to ensure that each person has focus and purpose in his or her daily work. Each deliverable will contribute to meeting the overall goals of GQM, Benefit-Risk Management, and Johnson & Johnson.
Strong focus on process	As a team, we will focus on understanding our processes and improving them on a continuous basis. We will strive to build relationships with our internal and external suppliers and customers and focus on the inputs and outputs of our processes.

Focus on talents of individuals	GQM management will focus on the talents of individuals, seeking to utilize their strengths. We will strive to assign responsibilities based on strengths while also providing opportunities for growth.
Flexibility	Each GQM employee will strive to be flexible as the organization and its processes change and grow. We will not be afraid of change, recognizing that change brings growth.

Strategic Step 2: Organize Your Organization for Quality

Organization of staff and work plays an important role in helping the team meet the imperatives of your management framework. Once you've identified the key outputs of your organization and the processes that support their delivery, you can assign process owners to each process. Even in a situation where several people follow the same processes, you can assign each person as the process owner for one of their shared processes. This gives accountability for processes to specific individuals within the organization. Once you have fully reviewed and discussed your management framework with your staff, you can begin to systematically go through some of the group activities outlined in Chapter 6 to begin building a collaborative culture that focuses on processes and customers. In my organization, each of my direct reports understands the processes for which he or she is responsible. I collaborate with each person at the beginning of every month to agree on what his or her specific process-related deliverables are for the month. These personal deliverables are either big-ticket deliverables that they and their teams may be responsible to deliver, or they may revolve around improvements to the processes for which they hold responsibility. Minor *routine* deliverables are not included. The process-related deliverables help the group to move forward while focusing on being productive and improving our efficiencies. At times, the deliverables can be those found in Table 8.3. At other times, they are even more specific. To provide an example, in Table 8.2 I have shared the list of deliverables for my direct reports for the month of February 2005. I have underlined key terms that support DMAIC activities and, therefore, the underlying concepts of Six Sigma.

Monthly deliverables for my direct reports are written on a whiteboard in my office. This further supports our organizational focus on deliverables. As I meet with each person throughout the month, whether formally or informally, the deliverables are there as a reference. This also provides me with a constant reminder and helps me to move the group forward. It is important to constantly keep the end goals in mind when using this management technique. Each month, the deliverables should serve to move each person toward accomplishing his or her long-term

Table 8.2   An Example of Monthly Deliverables

Direct Report	Deliverables
Direct Report 1, Assistant Director	Complete the SOP auditing plan and the job description binder auditing plan. Prepare to begin pilot in March. Complete first version of inspection tool kit and post to Web site
	Manage retirement of five SOPs
	Manage move of all SOP deviations to the Web site for accessibility
	Complete internal SOP audit plan and preparation to begin pilot in March
	Draft SOP on internal auditing
Direct Report 2, Senior Manager	Transition to managing Compliance staff
	Finalize SOP 208
	Manage significant progress on the development of the 12 SOPs currently under development
Direct Report 3, Manager	Distribute first Corrective Action Plan (CAP) update report and CAP Metrics Dashboard
	Facilitate approval of abc CAP
	Assign CAP items for xyz CAP and facilitate responses for 50 percent of CAP
	Finalize Periodic Safety Update Report (PSUR) process and metrics report
	Draft Project Plan for metrics on other key documents
Direct Report 4, Manager	Begin pilot process for review of serious expedited cases at site abc
	Distribute first single case quality Metric Dashboard
	Finalize medical content checklist and rating scale
	Present single case review pilot process at xzy site

goals, therefore accomplishing the overall goals of your organization. As you may gather from reading the monthly goals of my direct reports for February 2005, we happen to be in the improvement and control stages of the DMAIC cycle for most of our processes. When we were in the earlier stages, our goals were centered more around planning and information gathering via Voice of the Customer activities and collaboration. Mapping the "as-is" process was not applicable in some cases because we are implementing brand new processes. When there is no "as-is" process, you must brainstorm about how the new process would work based on the information gathered from customers, the expected deliverables, the available resources, and common sense. This is also an example of where collaboration with internal suppliers and customers is extremely valuable, particularly because you can develop a process together. Evaluating an "as-is" process with the goal of improving it is a bit more challenging, because your suppliers may be quite comfortable with the way things have always been. If approached correctly, customers are usually open to seeing improvements from you, but dealing with suppliers is a bit trickier. However, with a positive attitude and approach, challenging the status quo can have positive outcomes for all. The key is looking for win–win situations and presenting them as such. Make sure that you focus on the positives for the supplier. Rack your brains until you find the positives, present them to your suppliers, and see what happens! Be willing to hear their feedback and remember that continued collaboration is key.

I believe my strategy has been successful because I have applied Six Sigma concepts in a way that makes sense considering the goals, challenges, and expected deliverables of my own organization. When people in my personal organization become involved in a J&J Process Excellence project, they embrace the concepts presented because they understand them and have already applied them to their own work. Some say that traditional Six Sigma does not allow for innovation because a rigid process must be followed; however, what many people don't understand, including some Six Sigma Black Belts, is that the underlying principals of Six Sigma must also be applied to the Six Sigma methodology itself. You must look at the "as-is" process of Six Sigma and, within your environment and specific situation, ask yourself if you are adding extra steps and hand-offs that are unnecessary. If they aren't necessary, don't do them. It's that simple. Do what makes sense for your organization. Dare to be creative!

Strategic Step 3: Implement the DMAIC Cycle for Your Organization

Once you've assigned each organizational process to members of your staff and they have gained an understanding of the DMAIC model, you can begin working with them to gain an in-depth understanding of the "as-is" process and follow it through the DMAIC model toward improvement. Chapters 5 through 7 focused on process, customers, collaboration, and data-driven management activities that can be utilized as you and your staff move through the DMAIC model. Table 8.3 brings together all the various activities based on the cornerstone concepts underlying Six Sigma. It serves as a guide not only to demonstrate how the cornerstone concepts support the entire DMAIC cycle, but also as a template for how you can champion your own staff to build the organizational structure, tasks, goals, and outputs within a Six Sigma framework. The management framework that you've created and shared with them will support all of these activities because you will begin to build a culture that supports the use of Six Sigma tools and strategies. Remember, writing it all down on paper is only a very small piece of the puzzle. You must be a leader, showing through your daily actions that you intend to manage according to the framework. This means that outside of accomplishing the agreed upon goals for each employee, you will evaluate their performance based on *how* they accomplish those goals. They should understand that their daily actions and decisions should be based on the framework that you've laid out for them.

Table 8.3 pulls the Six Sigma activities from each DMAIC stage together into one picture. The table shows how, as a manager you can follow Six Sigma methodology within your own organization, focusing on the processes and deliverables that fall within your scope. However, by fine-tuning and utilizing your internal customer-focus and collaboration skills, you *can* reach beyond your scope, when necessary, to achieve even greater results. When interviewed, Paul Keller, vice president and senior consultant with Quality America, a Six Sigma consulting, training, and publishing firm, and coauthor of *Six Sigma Demystified*, said that the efforts of managers may be constrained by their authority over resources. He also stated that there is a real possibility that functional processes can become highly efficient at the expense of system optimization, especially if the functional managers do not have access to necessary customer input and/or the strategic plans for the organization. He said that these are risks that need to be recognized and mitigated. And I agree! This is why it is extremely critical that managers build relationships with their internal suppliers and customers. The goal should not be to improve your piece of the effort, process, or pie without full consideration of the surrounding circumstances. Major contributors to your surrounding circumstances will be the strategic plans and immediate goals and objectives of your suppliers, customers, supervisor, and the overall company. Each set of interests must be taken into account when making decisions, in particular those impacting your processes. Even as a manager trying to implement Six Sigma concepts on your own, the focus should be on the final external customer. If you keep your eyes and ears on your customers, you will continue on the right track. Ultimately, you can lead by example, regardless of whether your company has a strong Six Sigma program or has never heard of Six Sigma. As you establish a management framework and guide your staff through the applicable Six Sigma activities shown in Table 8.3, the secret is to maintain your focus on the data-driven management piece as well. Your data is key to showing others that you've made irrefutable progress and improvements by implementing your own Six Sigma-based initiative.

Strategic Step 4: Continuously Monitor and Improve Your Organization

The more you practice this type of management, the more comfortable it will become. Over time, your staff will understand and see the benefits of your strategic approach to managing their work. As an organization, you will come to appreciate that everyone does not have to come into the office every day to complete routine tasks and fight fires; the joy of work comes from building something bet-

Table 8.3   The DMAIC Model for Managers

DMAIC Stage	Six Sigma Cornerstone Concept	Activity	Deliverable(s)
Define	Process Focus (Chapter 5)	Identify key organizational deliverables Identify process to improve Map high-level process	Problem statement Process/Project scope Initial SIPOC with high-level process, defined scope, inputs and outputs
	Customer Focus and Collaboration (Chapter 6)	Identify suppliers and customers Identify stakeholders Conduct Voice of the Customer (VOC) exercise Create Kano Analysis	Kano Model
Measure	Process Focus (Chapter 5)	Identify process inputs and outputs	Final SIPOC
	Customer Focus and Collaboration (Chapter 6)	Identify Critical to Quality (CTQ) items, steps, etc. Create Operational Definitions	Prioritized CTQ List Prioritized Customer Needs List Operational Definitions
	Management by Data (metrics) (Chapter 7)	Identify key process measures Identify sampling strategy Collect process data Calculate sigma	Data Collection Plan Data forms and spreadsheets Process sigma
Analyze	Process Focus (Chapter 5)	Map the "as-is" process Brainstorm about the process Analyze the process flow Create detailed "to-be" process map	Detailed "as-is" process map Process Flow Analysis Detailed "to-be" process
	Customer Focus and Collaboration (Chapter 6)	Create Cause and Effect/Fishbone Diagram Determine value of process steps	Cause and Effect Analysis Value Analysis
	Management by Data (metrics) (Chapter 7)	Conduct Pareto Analysis Analyze histograms Analyze run charts	Data analysis for "as-is" process
Improve	Process Focus (Chapter 5)	Pilot process change(s)	Updated process map Pilot run information/learning
	Customer Focus and Collaboration (Chapter 6)	Brainstorm about solutions Evaluate impact versus effort Create Communication Plan Create Training Plan	Tree Diagram for Solutions Impact/Effort Matrix Communication Plan Training Plan

(Continues)

Table 8.3   (Continued)

DMAIC Stage	Six Sigma Cornerstone Concept	Activity	Deliverable(s)
Control	Process Focus (Chapter 5)	Institutionalize improvement	Standard Operating Procedure (SOP)
	Customer Focus and Collaboration (Chapter 6)	Share successes with stakeholders	Communicated project status
	Management by Data (metrics) (Chapter 7)	Create Metric Scorecard or Dashboard Create process monitoring tools	Process Control Plan Scorecard or Dashboard

ter—improving the status quo. This is what gives people a strong sense of accomplishment. To propel your team forward on a daily basis, it is up to you as their Champion to encourage them to perform to the best of their abilities. Part of this responsibility is making sure that they understand what is expected of them and holding them accountable for those achievements. There are numerous ways of doing this that include rewards and recognition throughout the year as well as yearly performance reviews and the associated outcomes.

When possible, it's a good idea to create a public forum to review the monthly objectives of each staff member or subgroup within your organization. I use monthly staff meetings for this purpose. Each of my direct reports reviews their progress at our monthly staff meetings, which is also attended by their reports. This helps focus the entire organization on the key monthly deliverables. This "report-out" is intended as a positive exercise where everyone is recognized for what they achieved within the month. Unfortunately, it does highlight situations where the work is not being completed; however, each person must take accountability for their work. If a monthly goal isn't met, the person explains why it wasn't met. Most times there is an acceptable reason, and the goal rolls to the following month. However, as a leader and Champion, it is important to take action when it's obvious to the entire group that an individual or subteam is not performing over time. The specific action needed is your call as the leader. If you allow nonperformers to float through while everyone else achieves their monthly and long-term goals, you will lose credibility.

Along with holding staff responsible to "report-out" monthly, it is also important to develop a rewards program within your organization. This can be as simple or as complicated as you want it to be. You may want to put something in place to recognize milestones achieved as a process owner moves through the DMAIC model, or you may want to present awards to those whose actions or achievements have exemplified a process focus, or a customer focus, or a focus on one of the other concepts within your management framework. The size of your organization will dictate how many monthly rewards or awards are appropriate. Use your creativity! Believe it or not, you do not need high-level support to create your own rewards and recognition program. The worst-case scenario is that you may have to shell out a few bucks of your own each month to buy small gifts for award winners. Many managers fail to take advantage of the rewards and recognition programs that already exist within their companies. Most of the larger companies already have budgets in place for this type of thing; just ask.

As you move forward with your efforts, you must keep the momentum going and continuously drive home the principles and focus of your management framework. Both enthusiasm and negativity are highly contagious in the workplace. It is your job as a manager to set the tone for the rest of your organization by *talking the talk* and *walking the walk*. In my opinion, being a Six Sigma Champion has even more meaning and purpose for the middle manager than it does for a high-level executive who has signed up for the job with the support of numerous Six Sigma professionals and consultants. You're not a figurehead; you are a leader who works in the trenches everyday, hand in hand with those in your organization. Keep your finger on the pulse!

The Bottom Line

- Creating a strategy that starts with a defined management framework within your own personal organization is an excellent training exercise. Not only will it hone your strategic planning and thinking skills, it will also help you achieve results in a consistent, documented, organized fashion that is visible to your staff and your supervisor.
- The first step toward leading a personal organization by using the Six Sigma cornerstone concepts is to create a management framework that will support your efforts.
- Organization of staff and work plays an important role in helping the team to meet the imperatives of your management framework.
- Once you've identified the key outputs of your organization and the processes that support their delivery, you can assign process owners to each process. This gives accountability for processes to specific individuals within the organization.
- Personal monthly deliverables are either big-ticket deliverables that your direct reports (and their staff) are responsible to deliver. The deliverables

may also revolve around improvements to the processes for which your direct reports hold responsibility. Having process-related deliverables helps the group to move forward while focusing on being productive and improving efficiencies.

■ You must look at the "as-is" process of Six Sigma and, within your environment and specific situation, ask yourself if you are adding extra steps and hand-offs that are unnecessary.

■ Once you've assigned each organizational process to members of your staff and they have gained an understanding of the DMAIC model, you can begin working with them to gain an in-depth understanding of the "as-is" process, and follow it through the DMAIC model toward improvement.

■ The management framework that you've created and shared with your staff will support all of these activities because you will begin to build a culture that supports the use of Six Sigma tools and strategies.

■ If you keep your eyes and ears on your customers, you will continue on the right track. Ultimately, you can lead by example regardless of whether your company has a strong Six Sigma program or has never heard of Six Sigma.

■ Your data is key to showing others that you've made irrefutable progress and improvements by implementing your own Six Sigma-based initiative.

■ When possible, it's a good idea to create a public forum to review the monthly objectives of each staff member or subgroup within your organization. This helps focus the entire organization on the key monthly deliverables.

Part Three

What Managers Can Learn from Others: A Black Belt's View

Chapter 9

Traditional Six Sigma: The 3,000-Foot View

A man who wants to lead the orchestra must turn his back on the crowd.
—James Crook

I hope by now you agree that it's time for middle management to give Six Sigma the attention it deserves. In doing so, we have to think outside the Six Sigma box. When I first heard about Six Sigma in the early 1990s, I was told that it was impossible to implement without high-level support. I would fail before I started. Well, I disagreed then and I disagree now. If you focus on implementing Six Sigma concepts within your own personal organization, you can change culture, reap the personal rewards of improved processes, and begin to impact the bottom line. Most Six Sigma leaders agree that it has been so successful because it has been management driven; however, quality should be the responsibility of each individual manager. For those of us who don't want to keep going to work every day to observe re-work, inefficiencies, and lack of common sense in our work environment, this methodology is available and will work. It seems that all the Six Sigma Black Belts and Champions have been so busy eagerly leading projects and ushering us through the DMAIC cycle that they may have missed a valuable point. We own the processes; those on the outskirts of the Six Sigma phenomenon need someone to tell us how to take charge of our quality so we don't have to wait for our CEO to declare a Six Sigma revolution! If he or she does, that's fantastic! But you don't have to wait. Be responsible for your own quality.

Parts 1 and 2 of this book provided a high-level review of the Six Sigma methodology and some of the common tools that can be used within your own scope of work. The underlying concepts of Six Sigma were defined and examples were provided. Finally, you were provided a high-level strategy for implementing Six Sigma concepts, methodology, and tools within your scope. With that learning in mind, Part 3 will, at the same time, go deeper and higher into the world of traditional Six Sigma. By digging deeper into the standard organizational set-up and functions of the key players, managers can begin to understand how implementation of the strategy described in Part 2 of the book can work. By taking a higher view, you can begin to understand the mindset of Six Sigma professionals—how you can emulate their passion for Six Sigma and work better with them once they do show up at your office door. What you are essentially encouraged to do is view Six Sigma (as described in this chapter) from a new angle. In doing so, you can take ownership and responsibility for the quality and efficiency (translated to cost savings) of your own organization and apply a new brand of Six Sigma to your workplace . . . one that makes sense for you—today.

A Brief History

Carl Frederick Gauss (1777–1855) introduced the use of six sigma as a measurement standard when he shared the concept of the normal curve. In the 1920s, Walter Shewhart was the first to use six sigma as a measurement standard in product variation when he showed that three sigma from the mean is the point where a process requires correction. The public record clearly shows that in the late 1970s, Dr. Mikel Harry, a senior staff engineer at Motorola's Government Electronics Group (GEG), began to experiment with problem solving through statistical analysis. According to Daniel T. Laux, president of Six Sigma Academy, by using Dr. Harry's methodology, GEG began to show dramatic results: its products were being designed and produced faster and more cheaply. Subsequently, Dr. Harry began to formulate a method for applying six sigma as a measurement standard throughout Motorola. His work culminated in a paper titled "The Strategic Vision for Accelerating Six Sigma within Motorola." He was later appointed head of the Motorola Six Sigma Research Institute and became the driving force behind Six Sigma as we know it now.

Dr. Mikel Harry and Richard Schroeder, an ex-Motorola executive, were responsible for creating the unique combination of change management and data driven methodologies that transformed Six Sigma from a simple quality measurement tool to the breakthrough business excellence philosophy it is today. Apparently, they had the charisma and the ability to educate and engage business leaders such as Bob Galvin of Motorola, Larry Bossidy of AlliedSignal (now Honeywell), and Jack Welch of GE. Together, Harry and Schroeder elevated Six Sigma from the shop floor to the boardroom with their drive and innovative ideas regarding entitlement, breakthrough strategy, sigma levels, and the roles for deployment of Black Belts, Master Black Belts, and Champions. Despite all this, there is some debate among Six Sigma practitioners as to who deserves credit for coining the term "Six Sigma." Many people who worked at Motorola at the time credit a studious mid-level engineer, Bill Smith. Smith died of a heart attack in the Motorola cafeteria in 1993 never knowing the scope of the craze and controversy he had touched off. Nevertheless, the term *Six Sigma* is a federally registered trademark of Motorola.

Six Sigma has evolved over time to become a way of doing business. Hundreds of companies around the world have now adopted Six Sigma.

Companies Now Using Six Sigma

Despite the long list of top companies embracing Six Sigma, many middle managers and small business owners are still just learning about it and trying to understand how it applies to them, how they can approach their senior management for support, or how they can apply it within their own scope.

As Geoff Tennant describes in his book, *Six Sigma: SPC and TQM in Manufacturing and Services*, "Six Sigma is many things, and it would perhaps be easier to list all the things that Six Sigma quality is *not*. Six Sigma can be seen as: a vision; a philosophy; a symbol; a metric; a goal; a methodology." The good news is that the Six Sigma vision, philosophy, symbol, metrics, goal, and methodology are not reserved for senior leadership, or GE, or J&J. Middle management, entrepreneurs, and small businessmen and businesswomen can also embrace Six Sigma and apply it within their worlds by thinking outside the Six Sigma box.

As more and more companies have implemented Six Sigma programs, there has been a groundswell of interest from quality management, engineering, and statistics professionals, as well as some functional managers, to become experts in the methodology. Facilitation of Six Sigma programs and projects has become a new career path for many, whether or not that was the intent of the original Six Sigma practitioners. People with years of experience in the quality field, Master's Degrees, and Ph.D.s in quality concepts, statistics, and engineering wishing to get involved have been required to pass the Black Belt certification to prove they have the capability to enter the world of Six Sigma. Although many of these people could pass the certification test with their hands tied behind their backs, they have had to compete for positions with less experienced and less educated Black Belts who underwent traditional Six Sigma training. (The usual training is four weeks of full-time classroom instruction and successful completion of one or two projects.) This is a testimony to how strongly industry is embracing the Six Sigma methodology.

There are distinct levels of Six Sigma expertise that can be achieved within a traditional Six Sigma organization. Companies organize in various ways to implement Six Sigma successfully; however, there are a handful of key functions deemed critical for success.

Six Sigma Companies

3M, A.B. Dick Company, Abbott Labs, Adolph Coors, Advanced Micro Devices, Aerospace Corp, Airborne, Alcoa, Allen Bradley, Allied Signal, Allstate, Amazon, American Express, Ampex, Apple Computers, Applied Magnetics, ASQC, Atmel, Bank of America, Baxter Pharmaseal, Beatrice Foods, Bell Helicopter, Boeing, Bombardier, Borden, Bosch, Bristol Meyers-Squibb, Bryn Mawr Hospital, Burlington Industries, Campbell Soup, Cellular 1, Chevron, Citicorp, City of Austin, Texas, City of Dallas, Texas, Canon, Clorox, Dannon, Defense Mapping Agency, Delnosa (Delco Electronics in Mexico), Digital Equipment Corp, Donnelley Logistics, Dow, Dupont, Eastman Kodak, Electronic Systems Center, Empak, Florida Department of Corrections, Ford Motor Company, GEC Marconi, General Dynamics, General Electric, Hazeltine Corp, Hewlett Packard, Holly Sugar, Honda, Honeywell, Intel, Intuit, Jaguar, Johnson & Johnson, Junior Achievement, Kaiser Aluminum, Kraft General Foods, Larson & Darby, Inc, Laser Magnetic Storage, Lear, Lenox China, Litton Data Systems, Lockheed Martin, Loral, Los Alamos National labs, Martin Marietta, Maytag, McDonnell Douglas, McKesson Corporation, Merix, Microsoft, Morton International, Mount Carmel Health System, Motorola, NASA, National Institute of Corrections, National Institute of Standards, National Semiconductor, Natural Gas Pipeline Company of America, Nokia, North Memorial Medical Center, Northrop Corp, PACE, Parkview Hospital, Pentagon, Pharmacia, Polaroid, PRC, Inc, Qualified Specialists, Raytheon, Ramtron Corp, Rockwell Int'l, Rohm & Haas, Seagate, Siemans, Society of Plastics Engineers, Solar Optical, Sony, Star Quality, Storage Tek, Sun Microsystems, Logic, Texaco, Texas Commerce Bank, Texas Department of Transportation, Texas Instruments, Toshiba, Ultratech Stepper, United States Air Force, United States Army, United Technologies, UPS, Vanguard Group, Verbatim, Virtua Health, Walbro Automotive, Walker Parking, Woodward Governor, Wyeth, Xerox

Executive Leader

According to traditional Six Sigma philosophy, Executive Leaders within the company must make the decision to implement Six Sigma and must publicly endorse it throughout the company. *This is the high-level support we're all told to seek.* Executive Leaders must reinforce the comprehensive scope of Six Sigma at every turn. This critical engagement of widespread participation throughout the company is critical for traditional Six Sigma. Traditional practitioners say that it's important for Six Sigma to be a companywide initiative and that it cannot be overemphasized. Employees must be rallied to the cause, and the targeted outcomes must become major company priorities.

Champion

In Six Sigma, Champions are advocates who fight for the cause and remove barriers to success, whether they are functional, financial, personal, or otherwise. They pave the way for Black Belts to do their jobs. If structured appropriately, Champions are also supposed to be process owners. This means that they are either functional executives or managers who have daily oversight and management of each critical element within the Six Sigma project. They need to report to senior management on project progress and they need to support their Six Sigma project teams. It's critical that Champions select projects that align with the company strategy and can be understood and embraced by project teams. Champions select Black Belt candidates and projects and ultimately establish clear, measurable goals for projects. They should be fully engaged in the process, using 20 to 30 percent of their time to ensure that progress is being made. According to Greg Brue, author of *Six Sigma for Managers*, Champions do not sit on the sidelines. Champions must be in the thick of the battle! Brue says that the Champion acts as an advocate and defender, as mentor and coach, and is ultimately responsible for project success. They must have a thorough understanding of the strategy and discipline of Six Sigma and be able to educate others on the topic.

Master Black Belt (MBB)

The Master Black Belt is an expert in all areas of Six Sigma. Within the company, the MBB serves as an official teacher for Champions and Black Belts. The MBB should be skilled at facilitating problem solving without taking over a project. MBBs are often assigned to a specific area or function within the company. It may be a functional area, such as human resources or legal, or a process-specific area, such as billing or tube rolling. MBBs work with the owners of the process (or Champions) to ensure that quality objectives and targets are set, plans are determined, progress is tracked, and education is provided. In the best Six Sigma organizations, Champions and MBBs work very closely and share information daily.

Black Belt (BB)

Black Belts are dedicated to assigned projects and work full time to drive project success. They lead the project team and are trained to dig into the chronic and high-impact issues and fix them using Six Sigma methodology and tools. Black Belts take the theory of Six Sigma and put it into action. They provide technical expertise in how to use Six Sigma tools to ensure that costly issues are corrected—and stay corrected. Black Belts can typically complete four to six projects per year with savings of approximately $230,000 per project. Black Belts also coach Green Belts on their projects, and while coaching may seem easy, it can require a significant amount of time and energy.

Charles Waxer, a highly regarded Six Sigma professional and frequent contributor to *iSixSigma Magazine*, offers a top 10 list of Black Belt qualities. According to Waxer, he chose to bullet the items rather than number them because numbering usually indicates that one point might be more valuable than another. In this case, he feels that all ten qualities are considered essential.

- *Customer Advocacy.* Black Belts should readily communicate the understanding that customers are always the recipients of processes, and that customers (both internal or external) are always the final judges of product or service quality.
- *Passion.* No cold fish are welcomed in Six Sigma. Black Belts must be self-motivated, have initiative, and have a positive personality. At times they are expected to be cheerleaders, to pick up the team and help them move forward productively. Passion also gives them fortitude to persevere, even when the going may get tough on a project.
- *Change Leadership.* Changing the organization and how business is accomplished may upset employees; change agents and change leaders have a way of accomplishing positive change while engendering support for the change.
- *Communication.* Black Belts are effective communicators, which is essential for the many roles they serve: trainers, coaches, and mentors. Black Belts should be able to speak clearly to all audiences (from shop floor employees to executive management). Understanding the various needs of audience members and tailoring the message to address their concerns is the mark of an effective communicator.
- *Business Acumen.* Black Belts are business leaders, not the quality managers of the past. As such, they should have business knowledge and the ability to display the linkage between projects and desired business results. How is a project making the company stronger competitively and financially?
- *Project Management.* Six Sigma is accomplished one project at a time. We should not lose sight of the fact that the Black Belt must manage projects from scope, requirements, resources, timeline, and variance perspectives. Knowledge of project management fundamentals and experience managing projects are essential.

- *Technical Aptitude.* The Black Belt candidate need not be an engineering or statistical graduate, but in some cases this is beneficial—provided the other top 10 qualities listed are also present. In all cases, a Black Belt is required to collect and analyze data for determining an improvement strategy. Without some technical aptitude (computer software literacy and analytical skills), the Black Belt will be frustrated in this role.
- *Team Player and Leader.* Black Belts must possess the ability to lead, work with teams, be part of a team, and understand team dynamics. In order to effectively lead a team, a Black Belt must be likeable, get along with people, have good influencing skills, and motivate others.
- *Results Oriented.* Black Belts are expected to perform and produce tangible financial results for the business. They must be hard working and quick to demonstrate success.
- *Fun.* Black Belts should enjoy their jobs if they are passionate about them. By having fun, you encourage others to do the same.

Managers should consider these qualities as critical to the success of their own implementation efforts. In essence, you are not only the Champion for your team but also the Black Belt. This may sound overwhelming, but when you carefully consider the qualities listed above, as well as those stated for a strong Champion, you will see that these are all qualities that make good business leaders. In your management position, you should strive to be a strong leader. Implementing the concepts and methodologies of Six Sigma is merely creating a strategy for how you will manage your personal organization. This is how you can use Six Sigma itself as a tool for implementing and ensuring business excellence within your personal organization.

Green Belt (GB)

Green Belts are functional experts who assist Black Belts on projects. They are employees trained in Six Sigma who spend a portion of their time completing projects, but maintain their regular work role and responsibilities. Depending on their workload, they can spend anywhere from 10 to 50 percent of their time on their project(s). Black Belts transfer their knowledge of Six Sigma to Green Belts so that they can begin to use it in even narrower applications. Theoretically, as the Six Sigma quality program evolves, employees will begin to include the Six Sigma methodology in their daily activities, and it will no longer take up a percentage of their time. It will be the way their work is accomplished 100 percent of the time. Within your own organization, your staff is basically filling this position.

There is another role that continuously pops up in the world of Six Sigma that should not be ignored and may hit close to home for managers. It is the role of the *process owner.* In Part 2 of this book, we established that process owners are responsible for a specific process. In a traditional sense, the label of *process owner* is given to the person in charge of a function, or the Champion. For example, in the legal department there is usually one person in charge—maybe the VP of Legal—who's the process owner. There may be a chief marketing officer for your business—that's the process owner for marketing. But depending on the size of your business and core activities, you will have process owners at lower levels of your personal organizational structure. If yours is a credit card company with processes covering billing, accounts receivable, audit, billing fraud, etc., you wouldn't have the process owner be only the chief financial officer, you would want to go much deeper into the organization where the work is being accomplished. Therefore, process owners can be and should be established within your scope of responsibility.

Some Six Sigma consultants are earning seven figure salaries; CEOs of large companies are claiming billions of dollars saved; conferences, books, and seminars are popping up everywhere; and Six Sigma utilizes the basic concepts found in most major quality management philosophies. So is Six Sigma just the latest management buzzword, or is Six Sigma a quality management program that really works? Six Sigma does have a few new twists. These new twists make Six Sigma different enough to exist on its own and are what makes Six Sigma work much better than any other quality methodology of the past.

According to the International Society of Six Sigma Professionals, Six Sigma only appears to be a little different in terms of quality tools, techniques, and principles, but from a global perspective it's a whole new animal. Table 9.1 shows some of the reasons why (*in order of importance*) and how these differences relate to managers' efforts to implement Six Sigma.

Thomas Pyzdek, author of several top-selling Six Sigma books, including *The Six Sigma Handbook* and *The Six Sigma Project Planner*, shares some additional reasons why Six Sigma stands out from other quality management philosophies, including Total Quality Management—an approach used primarily in the 1980s:

- Six Sigma extends the use of the improvement tools to cost, cycle time, and other business issues. In other words, it goes beyond the strict use of statistical tools for manufacturing and other traditional applications. This means you can apply it in your world!

- Six Sigma discards the majority of the quality toolkit. It keeps a subset of tools that range from the basic to the advanced. Training focuses on using the tools to achieve tangible business results, not on theory. This means that traditional Six Sigma focuses on doing what makes sense, and your program should too. Managers can use Six Sigma tools that fall toward the basic category with success. The key is choosing the right approach and showing business results.

Table 9.1 Key Reasons Why Six Sigma Differs from Other Quality Approaches

Key Reason	Brief Explanation	What This Means for Your Self-Empowered Program
Top Leadership Support	Past GE CEO Jack Welch is quoted for telling employees that if they wanted to get promoted, they'd better become Black Belts. Universal cost-oriented metrics and the new level of competition that Six Sigma provides easily acquire top-level support. Some argue that the only addition that Six Sigma provides is the way top management is treating it. What's really important is that CEOs are seriously supporting large improvement projects run by highly trained business super stars. Top leadership commits to using Six Sigma as a management framework, and then they stand behind it.	It is critical that managers implementing Six Sigma establish and commit to a strong management framework based on the concepts and methodologies of Six Sigma. You must stand behind your commitment!
Highly Trained Players with a Solid Organizational Framework	Six Sigma has a set of critical team players dedicated to the effort. (These are the roles discussed in the text.) Six Sigma companies organize for quality.	Managers should also organize for quality. While you may not have Green Belts and Black Belts, you can designate process owners and hold them accountable to drive process improvements within your scope based on the underlying concepts of Six Sigma.
Training Like Never Before	The training is heavily statistical, project management and problem solving oriented. Training costs of approximately $15,000 to $25,000 per Black Belt are well justified by the savings per project.	It is critical to train your staff on the basics of what you are trying to accomplish. There are creative ways to train and mentor staff aside from costly programs. Encourage them to read specific books, discuss and brainstorm about the concepts and tools highlighted in this book, and collaborate to determine how your team can apply them to the day-to-day work. Also, take advantage of any training budgets and programs your company may have in place. Create your own strategy for getting the message across to staff as a *(Continues)*

Table 9.1   (*Continued*)

Key Reason	Brief Explanation	What This Means for Your Self-Empowered Program
		team and as individuals. First and foremost, set a strong example for them to follow.
New Metrics	Use of metrics unlike anything ever used before. Metrics now tie customer Critical to Quality needs with what is measured by the company, and also compare processes within the company with one another using a single scale called DPMO (defects per million opportunities).	As a manager, maintain your focus on data-driven management!
Much Better Use of Teams	Very efficient use of highly trained, cross-functional, and empowered teams to locate and make improvements. Black Belts are also trained team-efficiency experts.	View your personal organization as a team. Strengthen your team! Take time to build the team, seeking to have a common understanding of the organizational goals and a common vision. Your documented management framework can aid in bringing the team together.
A New Corporate Attitude/Culture	Implementation of Six Sigma creates a new environment that naturally promotes the creation of continuous improvement efforts.	As you roll out your management framework, manage based on the underlying concepts of Six Sigma, and work through the DMAIC cycle, you will foster a new environment focused on continuous improvement within your own organization.

- Six Sigma integrates the goals of the organization as a whole into the improvement effort. Sure, quality is good, says Pyzdek, but not independent of other business goals. Six Sigma creates top-level oversight to assure that the interests of the entire organization are considered. This is why managers must understand the goals of the broader organization and use customer focus and collaboration to build strong ties with internal suppliers and customers. This is what makes you a Champion for your personal organization; this is your responsibility.
- Six Sigma strives for world-class performance. The Six Sigma standard is 3.4 failures per million opportunities. It goes beyond looking at errors.

The best of the Six Sigma firms try to meet or exceed their customer's expectations 999,996.4 times out of every million encounters. This calls for commitment and passion! As a manager, you've got to have it, show it, and foster it within your personal organization. This is not always an easy thing to do, but the rewards are there to be found if you're willing to put forth the effort.

According to Pyzdek, who has worked with organizations that have implemented Total Quality Management and Six Sigma as well, successful programs of both types *look* very much alike. But by clearly *defining* this "look," Six Sigma makes it easier for organizations to succeed by providing a clear roadmap to success. Organizations are more willing to invest the effort if they know that a pot of gold awaits them at the end. Creating a Six Sigma "look" for managers is also important for successful implementation. This "look" must be fashioned after the "look" of traditional Six Sigma, but it must make sense and apply to manager-level responsibilities within the organization.

The Bottom Line

- If you focus on implementing Six Sigma concepts within your own personal organization, you can change culture, reap the personal rewards of improved processes, and begin to impact the bottom line.
- View Six Sigma from a new angle. In doing so, you can take ownership and responsibility for the quality and efficiency (translated to cost savings) of your own organization and apply a new brand of Six Sigma to your workplace...one that make sense for you today.
- Despite the long list of top companies embracing Six Sigma, many middle managers and small business owners are still just learning about it and trying to understand how it applies to them, how they can approach their senior management for support, or how they can apply it within their own scopes.
- There are distinct levels of Six Sigma expertise that can be achieved within a traditional Six Sigma organization. Companies organize in various ways to successfully implement Six Sigma; however, there are a handful of key functions deemed critical for success.
- According to traditional Six Sigma philosophy, *Executive Leaders* within the company must make the decision to implement Six Sigma and must publicly endorse it throughout the company. *This is the high-level support we're all told to seek.*
- In Six Sigma, *Champions* are advocates who fight for the cause and work to remove barriers to success, whether they are functional, financial, personal, or otherwise.

- *Black Belts* are dedicated to assigned projects and work full time to drive project success. They lead the project team and are trained to dig into the chronic and high-impact issues and fix them using Six Sigma methodology and tools.
- In essence, the self-empowered manager is not only the Champion for your team but also the Black Belt. This may sound overwhelming, but when you carefully consider the key qualities for Black Belts, as well as those stated for a strong Champion, you will see that these are all qualities that make good business leaders.
- *Green Belts* are functional experts who assist Black Belts on projects. They are employees trained in Six Sigma who spend a portion of their time completing projects, but maintain their regular work role and responsibilities.
- In a traditional sense, the label of *process owner* is given to the person in charge of a function or the Champion. But depending on the size of your personal organization and core activities, you will have process owners at lower levels of the organizational structure.
- Creating a Six Sigma "look" for managers is important for successful implementation. This "look" must be fashioned after the "look" of traditional Six Sigma, but it must make sense and apply to manager-level responsibilities within the organization.

Chapter 10

Learning from Traditional Six Sigma Applied to Manufacturing

When you read, read! Too many students just half read....The art of memory is the art of understanding.
—Roscoe Pound, Dean Emeritus, Harvard Law School

Odds are you've read case studies about Six Sigma successes. You may have read them in magazines or other Six Sigma books, or you may have heard about them at conferences or from Internet sources. Obviously, these success stories provide a wealth of information on how traditional Six Sigma programs work, the key players involved, and the successful outcomes. In this chapter, you will read about three manufacturing companies, Raytheon, 3M, and Honeywell, which have embraced Six Sigma and have mature programs. The incredible results they achieved in their manufacturing units inspired them to use Six Sigma throughout their companies. They branched into nonmanufacturing areas, where they continued to see success. Just as these companies expanded the use of Six Sigma from manufacturing into nonmanufacturing departments, Six Sigma concepts and methodology can be moved to various *levels* within organizations. These companies decided that Six Sigma could apply to areas other than manufacturing because they didn't want to limit the use of Six Sigma; they began to understand that the concepts and methodology could apply to all functions within an organization. With determination and creative thinking, they figured out just how to do it. Using this same mindset within our own personal organizations, managers at all levels can also take advantage of the benefits of Six Sigma by continuing to expand its use.

Each case study presented in this chapter focuses on one of the Six Sigma cornerstone concepts of process focus, customer focus and collaboration, and data-driven management. As you read each case study, challenge yourself to look for these elements and how the companies used them to improve their business. In addition, think deeply about how you may be able to apply their techniques to your own scope of work. The answers and ideas that surface will be different for each person, based on the type of business, the size and scope of your personal organization, and how determined you are to embrace the key concepts. Be creative and consider what you've learned in Parts 1 and 2 of this book.

3M: Process Focus

Although 3M implemented Six Sigma companywide in 2001, the $16 billion international conglomerate had already been using the statistical analysis tools of the process since 1995. It was then that 3M introduced statistical analysis to improve yield, cycle time, and quality of the manufacture of flexible circuits. Since 2001, 3M has trained more than 30,000 employees in Six Sigma, with plans to train all salaried employees as Green Belts by year-end 2004. In that time, 3M has closed, or completed, 11,000 Six Sigma projects and has another 12,000 underway as of early 2005.

CEO Jim McNerney's arrival at 3M in 2001 was the impetus behind the company's adoption of Six Sigma. At that time, the company was using several process improvement and quality programs, one of which was Six Sigma. But McNerney felt strongly that "the entire company [needed to] adopt one [methodology], so that we could develop a common language...so that we could leverage our size," he said in a 2004 *Industry Week* interview. "...Six Sigma was something I was familiar with. I believed in it [and] a number of people in the company [also] did, so that was sort of the one we all decided to go after."

According to the company, Six Sigma also "provides a common approach to process improvement throughout the company, provides a common language globally, develops transferable leadership skills at all levels of the company, and encourages a focus on tangible, measurable results and customer satisfaction."

3M's Six Sigma guide states, "At 3M, Six Sigma methods are used to analyze and improve the key processes that affect our growth, costs, cash, and customers. The results are faster commercialization and shorter cycle times, increased productivity, improved cost structures, better utilization of cash resources, and, most importantly, higher levels of customer satisfaction."

The company divides the program into three components: goals, measures, and projects. Its goals include cost, growth, cash, and customer. Measures consist of better yield, faster rate, lower cost, and less waste. Projects are initiated to achieve more valued features, reduced cycle time, increased performance, lowered inventory, fewer defects, and improved yield.

To achieve breakthrough improvements, 3M relies on the DMAIC approach. "Once a process improvement project is defined, a Six Sigma team will systematically measure, analyze, improve, and control that process in their drive for defect reduction, process improvement, and customer satisfaction."

3M's executive management team drives the company's Six Sigma efforts, but responsibility for implementing Six Sigma cascades through the organization. There are several levels of involvement in Six Sigma, ranging from Six Sigma Directors to Green Belts. Six Sigma Directors are full-time leaders who report to senior executives and are responsible for deploying Six Sigma within their units. Champions are leaders who support Six Sigma projects by "identifying improvement opportunities and ensuring adequate resources and support for Six Sigma teams," according to 3M's guide. Six Sigma Coaches are tool experts who coach and support Master Black Belts and Black Belts as needed. Master Black Belts are full-time leaders responsible for Six Sigma strategy, training, mentoring, deployment, and results, as well as leading and supporting Black Belts. Black Belts are full-time Six Sigma experts who serve two-year terms, leading process improvement teams. Green Belts are salaried employees who have received Six Sigma training and who are responsible for using that knowledge to complete projects in their individual job functions.

The company focused first on its factories, says McNerney, working on yield, scrap, and rework, and succeeded in boosting productivity significantly. "Then we moved into our backrooms: finance, and HR, and our customer service organizations," says McNerney, where productivity also climbed. Once employees embraced Six Sigma, 3M moved to convince customers to adopt Six Sigma to address their key business issues. Between 2003 and 2004, when customer collaborations began, 3M initiated 160 customer projects.

But in 2001, Six Sigma began with a challenge from McNerney to achieve a 5 to 8 percent annual growth from internally developed new products, which he dubbed "3M Acceleration." To enable this level of growth, management created the 2×/3× process, which is designed to double the number of new ideas considered for commercialization and triple the commercial impact of products that are ultimately launched. The introduction of the 2×/3× process companywide served to spread the responsibility for innovation and new product introduction across all functions, rather than limiting it to R&D, points out an article in *Research-Technology Management* magazine.

While 3M is a staunch Six Sigma supporter, in some cases the company has modified or adapted Six Sigma processes to meet its own needs for innovation, incorporating them in their Design for Six Sigma (DFSS) efforts. Some examples include:

- Screening early-stage ideas as "revolutionary," "evolutionary," or "overlooked." How each idea is categorized determines its strategy and funding model.
- Developing a question set called "won/lost," which helps analyze past product successes and failures to provide a perspective on new ideas and projects.
- Analyzing ideas using the "real, win, worth" tool 3M created. This tool evaluates new ideas, asking: "Is the opportunity real?" "Can we win at it?" "Is it worth it?"

One of the byproducts of the introduction of the $2\times/3\times$ process was the reorganization of its corporate research resources in 2003. The company's 900 researchers were reassigned, with 400 who had been working in 3M's corporate technology centers deployed to the R&D units of the company's seven business groups. The remaining 500 researchers were assigned to one of four sections: materials, processes, software/electronics/mechanical systems, and analytical. The company's 12 technology centers were dissolved and one corporate research lab formed to support the company's efforts, which was staffed with 100 new researchers from outside the United States. The addition of those new researchers brought 3M's research team to a total of 1,000 scientists and engineers, which is funded by a $1.1 billion annual budget.

Boosting its research efforts has been one of 3M's focuses through Six Sigma, but cutting costs and increasing sales are others. At 3M Canada, Six Sigma helped to reduce the sales cycle on the company's Scotchlite Reflective Materials. The project involved shortening the time between the initial sales visit and the completion of a written specification that incorporated Scotchlite Reflective Materials into the customer's safety garments, which helps enhance visibility and safety in the workplace. Because the sales process involves both the customer and the garment manufacturers, it typically took eight months to finalize an order, which included writing the specifications, prototyping garments, and conducting field trials, explains Brenda Ackerman, a Six Sigma Black Belt at 3M, in a case study she authored for *Simulation Success* magazine.

The goal of the project was to reduce the sales cycle by 40 percent, to five months, by developing procedures and tools that would accelerate the specification writing process and increase the total number written.

The first step was to map out the sales process, which the team did and which helped identify six key areas where improvement was required in order to reduce the cycle time. The next step was to run a Design of Experiments on the process, where the solution is tested, but waiting an entire sales cycle would take eight months and the team only had six remaining to complete the project. The answer was ProcessModel, a computer model that simulated the sales cycle. "We were able to test possible solutions in just minutes and see how changes or a combination of changes would affect the process. Simulation gave us the ability to change various parameters in the sales cycle to enable us to accomplish our goal," says Ackerman.

The simulation mirrored the existing process and allowed the team to identify where delays were occurring in the process and to monitor the results of changing certain parameters. ProcessModel helped the team develop several recommendations for eliminating the delays. It also bolstered the team's confidence to proceed with the recommendations following the simulation, reports Ackerman. The result of the project trimmed the sales cycle beyond the original five-month goal, which also, presumably, increased sales.

In total, Six Sigma contributed to 3M's $400 million increase in operating income in 2004, reports CEO Jim McNerney in the *Wall Street Journal*. McNerney also expects the company's operating income to increase by the same amount in 2005.

Raytheon: Customer Focus and Collaboration

Several years ago, Raytheon Company, based in Sudbury, Massachusetts, implemented Six Sigma companywide in an effort to increase profits by streamlining manufacturing operations, improving quality, and reducing defects. Through such efforts, Raytheon achieved cycle time reductions, yield improvements, and more effective inventory management, all of which have helped drive down total costs.

But the company recognized that in order to reap all the benefits of such an approach, its suppliers needed to buy into the Six Sigma process as well. As a result, in 2001, Raytheon developed and introduced the Raytheon Six Sigma for Suppliers program, designed to train and assist supply chain members in using Six Sigma tools to improve their own internal processes. By rolling out such a program to suppliers, Raytheon's goal was to gain a sustainable competitive advantage.

The Suppliers program consists of six problem-solving steps:

1. Visualize—identify supplier candidates
2. Commit—define objectives and resources
3. Prioritize—rank baseline opportunities
4. Characterize—analyze selected opportunities
5. Improve—implement projects
6. Achieve—document and realize improvements

"Six Sigma is something we associate with manufacturing. It provides companies with a way to look at cash flows, make sure deliveries are on time, and that quality issues are addressed," says Collin Reeves, a supplier technical consultant at Raytheon in a 2001 *EBN* article. "But we've taken that process and applied it with our suppliers." In doing so, Raytheon and its partners lower implementation costs on collaborative projects, estimate the savings of such endeavors, calculate the pay-back ratio, and define implementation milestones.

Much of the number crunching is completed during two-day workshops Raytheon hosts with its suppliers, many of which are military systems vendors rather than component makers. In order to participate in such workshops, suppliers must be willing to share a significant amount of financial data with Raytheon, including labor, material, factory overhead, and administrative expense figures. With that information in hand, the two organizations calculate the costs associated with each step in the project's process.

Six Sigma is evident everywhere within Raytheon. It is used to identify and address improvement opportunities in virtually every unit of the company. One such unit, Raytheon Aircraft Company (RAC), applied Six Sigma principles to address its excess work-in-process inventory in an effort to reduce costs and improve its financial position. In late 2002, the director of the Hawker 800XP jet aircraft, which had been found to account for 25 percent of the work-in-process at RAC, led a session of his direct reports, first-line supervisors, and a representative from each core function to identify problems and plan for improvements in the coming year.

It soon became clear that to improve efficiency and reduce work-in-process, it was necessary to reconfigure the assembly process. To proceed with such a massive undertaking, RAC obtained senior management support and then began to train 150 employees in Six Sigma techniques. Those employees were then divided into five project teams, each led by a Raytheon Six Sigma expert. The teams consisted of an assembly process team, which outlined the sequence required to build an aircraft; a "lean" team, which developed a more efficient material flow and relocated the stockroom to be closer to the assembly line; a material team, which prepared a delivery schedule that ensured all work-in-process would be removed from the value chain; a quality team, which developed a Hawker Quality Process; and a training team, for reacting to daily production problems in a timely manner.

The new seven-station Hawker assembly line debuted in July 2003, providing an immediate $27.5 million in cash flow benefit and a net operating profit of $2 million per year, with the possibility of greater results over time.

Internal collaborations between functional units and project teams are common within Raytheon, but the company's commitment to communicating the benefits of Six Sigma extends beyond its own organization to include suppliers and external customers. In some cases, such as with the U.S. Air Force, a collaboration yielded immediate financial benefits for both organizations.

In working with the U.S. Air Force to improve the production process for its AIM-9X Sidewinder missile and reduce total costs, Raytheon used Quality Function Deployment (QFD), a technique for translating the customer's wants and needs into company requirements, and Design for Manufacture and Assembly (DFMA), a method for reducing cycle time at manufacturing stages as well as improving producibility and maintainability. To that end, Raytheon held more than 25 workshops with the Air Force and key suppliers to identify opportunities for improvement and to ensure that the company was capable of making such changes.

Through information sharing and Six Sigma analysis, Raytheon was able to reduce the life-cycle costs of the AIM-9X missile by $1.2 billion.

Though the results of this effort were evident in the short term, in other situations, as with the National Science Foundation (NSF), the collaboration goal is long-term relationship building and information sharing. The results, however, are equally powerful and valuable.

NSF approached Raytheon's Polar Services in 2002 about participating in a Six Sigma project designed to reduce the number of expensive and risky medical evacuations taking place from NSF research stations in Antarctica. One such evacuation, in 2001, cost more than $450,000.

The joint team held a kick-off meeting at NSF and started by identifying six key areas that were top priorities. These included:

- Recruitment, selection, and retention
- Medical screening
- Psychological screening
- Accidents and injuries
- Medical capabilities
- Medical evacuation process

Subteams were then formed, each dedicated to addressing one of the six priorities and led by a Raytheon content expert and a Six Sigma expert. Although many Six Sigma tools were used during the project, one of the most important was a benchmarking survey with other organizations that deploy people to live and work in remote regions.

Through this collaboration the team made significant progress in four areas:

- Creating a health-and-safety-conscious culture to reduce safety incidents on the ice and provide occupational medicine and diagnostic training for medical staff
- Improvements in recruiting, selecting, and retaining high quality employees
- Improvements in access to medical help and treatment tools, through a telemedicine upgrade, clinic equipment modernization, and a pharmacy database
- Redefining the medical evacuation process and sharing information between Raytheon and NSF's Psychological Screening Team

With a few short months, NSF saw results. The total recordable injury rate fell 47 percent during the first six months, at a savings of $273,000, while medical evacuations dropped 22 percent and worker compensation claims declined by approximately $1.2 million in the first year.

Honeywell: Data-Driven Management

Honeywell International, Inc. is credited with being one of the forerunners of Six Sigma, having "invented and refined Six Sigma," along with Motorola and GE, when it was Allied Signal, according to Charles Waxer of iSixSigma. Allied Signal merged with Honeywell in 1999 but began deploying Six Sigma practices in 1994. Honeywell itself introduced Six Sigma in 1998.

Today the Morristown, New Jersey, company employs approximately 100,000 employees who work in 95 countries. Although most companies operate at about the three sigma level, which equates to 66,810 defects per million, or 93 percent error-free, Honeywell is approaching four sigma, or 6,200 defects per million, with a goal of six sigma and 3.4 defects per million.

CEO Larry Bossidy introduced Six Sigma at Allied Signal as a catalyst for change. "Our Six Sigma program was designed, from the very beginning, to produce business results by changing our culture, improving our work behaviors, expanding our skill sets, and transforming our mindsets," he explains in a *Six Sigma Forum* article. It was also key to getting the combined companies speaking the same language, namely, numbers. Four years later, as Honeywell, Six Sigma was deemed a success as the company calculated more than $2 billion in cost savings due to the methodology and 988 percent growth in its stock price.

From the beginning, Bossidy was committed to Six Sigma, which is part of the reason the program has been so successful. "He also painted a clear picture of the opportunity Six Sigma presented, and he tied it specifically to a definitive business purpose. He didn't just tell us to do Six Sigma; he made it very clear our business could not thrive without it," says Robert Papandria of Honeywell in a *Six Sigma Forum* interview. Six Sigma leaders were selected and assigned to each business unit, and measurement tools were chosen to measure each unit's progress. Even today, each business must report monthly using a common set of performance metrics.

What makes Honeywell a stand-out is its staunch commitment to sticking with Six Sigma, even in the face of economic downturns. Explains another Honeywell employee, Bill Ramsey, "In businesses under cost pressure, the response is not to cut back on Six Sigma resources but to increase them so we can drive the necessary growth and productivity," he reports in *Six Sigma Forum*.

Honeywell's initiative, called Six Sigma Plus, is a combination of AlliedSignal's and Honeywell's individual quality management systems. Using Six Sigma Plus, the company approaches each improvement project using the DMAIC process:

- Define the customer-critical parameters.
- Measure how the process performs.
- Analyze the causes of the problems.
- Improve the process to reduce defects and variation.
- Control the process to ensure continued, improved performance.

Additionally, the company relies frequently on several Six Sigma tools. These include:

- Brainstorming, where open thinking is encouraged and employees build on one another's ideas
- Flowcharts and process maps, which help a team identify the order of events in providing a product or service, discover problems, and compare the ideal workflow to what is currently occurring
- Pareto charts, which help identify the critical issues that directly impact cost and customer satisfaction
- Root cause analysis, which helps determine the underlying, true cause of a problem
- Control charts, which help team members observe and improve process performance

Using these tools, Honeywell has made significant progress in reducing costs and increasing revenues. For instance, an industrial control team achieved a 500 percent increase in revenue, which translated to several million dollars in operating profits, by developing a new family of chips and components for the data communications market, according to *Quality Digest* magazine. Honeywell Aerospace Services used Six Sigma Plus to reduce component repair time by 43 percent over two years, helping to boost Honeywell's revenue by $47 million and achieve productivity improvements valued at $900,000. A systems team in Mexicali, Mexico, focused on teardown and cleaning processes, reducing cycle time by 92 percent and space by 51 percent, and eliminated the need for chemicals to be used in cleaning operations, thereby saving the company $400,000. And Honeywell's travel department moved 93 percent of the company's airline bookings online, reaching an 83 percent touchless rate—only 17 percent of reservations were made with the help of a travel agent—and netting more than $6 million in savings, according to *Business Travel News*.

Now that the company has demonstrated an internal adoption of a Six Sigma mindset, Honeywell has turned its attention to its vendors. In some businesses,

Honeywell has outsourced portions of its manufacturing process to external suppliers, thereby relying on those suppliers to maintain Honeywell's lofty quality goals. Some have fared better than others, so Honeywell stepped in to improve quality at every point in the production process.

One step in that process was to establish an ongoing system for documenting supplier performance to spot problems before they impact the production process. Now, instead of reviewing supplier evaluations annually, the Web-based supplier performance system provides monthly metrics, which help both Honeywell and the suppliers see how they're doing.

Suppliers' scores range from 4 to 20 points, with 20 being the best. Suppliers with scores below 10 are expected either to provide a plan for improving their performance, to be working closely with a Honeywell quality and supplier development engineer to bring up their score, or to put a transition plan in place to redirect work to other, more qualified, suppliers.

In cases where Honeywell engineers began to work with suppliers, such as Wong's-CMAC in Mexico, the improvements were striking. Wong's-CMAC coats printed circuit boards with a substance designed to protect the boards in corrosive environments. In 2001, however, Honeywell found it was seeing areas with coating that weren't supposed to be coated, and other areas with coating missing or showing bubbles. To address the problem, Honeywell began to work with the company.

The team started by creating a detailed process map. Next, they listed all the Critical to Quality (CTQ) parameters and rated each step in the process by how likely it was to impact the CTQ. For instance, explains Dan Fink, Honeywell's manager of supplier quality and development in a *Purchasing* article, a CTQ parameter in this case might be thickness of coating. A process step of "remove part from box" gets a lower CTQ rating than a step of "mix liquid coating."

Once the process map was completed, the team conducted a Failure Modes and Effects Analysis (FMEA) on the highest rated steps to determine where to focus their attention. Early on, it became obvious that quality inspectors at Honeywell were using different criteria than the Wong's-CMAC inspectors. So they conducted a Kappa study, where all the inspectors sampled a known universe of parts and the differences in their results were compared to identify the inspectors in need of training. The study was so effective, says a Honeywell team member, that Wong's-CMAC continues to do it monthly to make sure its own inspectors are calibrated internally.

Another effective tool was the creation of visual work instructions for Wong's-CMAC employees. The diagrams of the printed circuit boards featured precise measurements and arrows indicating where the masking should be located on each board. Being able to refer to the diagram helped improve the consistency and reliability of the masking operations, which improved the coating quality.

When Honeywell began its work with Wong's-CMAC, the company's quality performance was 3.2 sigma, or 44,565 defects per million. For the three months ending December 2001, the company performed at six sigma—a dramatic improvement in a short period of time.

Although experts agree that Six Sigma will never be a quick fix for any company, there is a significant long-term upside. iSixSigma estimates that the savings from Six Sigma projects can range from 1.2 to 4.5 percent of revenue per year. For Honeywell, a $23 billion company in 2003, those savings add up to between $276 million and more than $1 billion. Per year.

Chapter 11

Learning from Traditional Six Sigma Applied to Nonmanufacturing or Service Industries

Any piece of knowledge I acquire today has a value at this moment exactly proportioned to my skill to deal with it. Tomorrow, when I know more, I recall that piece of information and use it better.

—Mark Van Doren

As you've learned, Six Sigma continues to develop beyond manufacturing. This happened first in manufacturing companies that wanted to expand their use of Six Sigma. They began to take the concepts into their supporting departments, such as sales, finance, and human resources. As the resulting success stories began to find their way into the literature and presentations at the numerous quality conferences springing up everywhere, other industries began to notice. This chapter highlights three of those industries, sharing cases studies from:

- Intuit—representing the software industry
- Bank of America—representing the financial industry
- North Memorial Medical Center in Robbinsdale, Minnesota—representing the healthcare industry

These industries have also benefited from senior management changes that have introduced Six Sigma into their organizations.

Just as in Chapter 10, each of the case studies presented focuses on one of the cornerstone concepts of process focus, customer focus and collaboration, and data driven management. Depending on your industry, you may identify with one case study more than others; however, continue to read with a creative hat on, relating their challenges and strategies to your own scope of work.

Intuit: Focusing on Process

Most companies can cite a particular day and time when their Six Sigma efforts kicked into high gear. At Intuit, that day was in early 2000, when Steve Bennett joined Intuit as CEO. Intuit is perhaps best known for its leading business and financial management tools, such as Quicken, QuickBooks, and TurboTax software. Founded in 1983, the company had an annual revenue of nearly $1.9 billion in 2004 and nearly 7,000 employees in the United States, Canada, and the United Kingdom.

Arriving at Intuit from GE, where Six Sigma is thoroughly ingrained in the culture, Bennett brought with him a passion for process excellence that spread throughout the company. But it didn't happen overnight. Tracie Lofgren, director of Process Excellence at Intuit, explains that the business went through four phases in its adoption of the Six Sigma methodology, which Intuit refers to as Process Excellence.

Intuit first targeted its call centers, a transaction-oriented environment within sales and technical support. This is where it proved the theory of the case. Then it moved to deploy Six Sigma resources functionally, dedicating Process Excellence resources to every business and function across Intuit. The primary purpose here was to begin, top down, to shape the mindset of Intuit's leaders and put fundamental operating mechanisms in place to ensure sustained impact. "We went deep, then we went broad," says Lofgren. Then it was time to "put points on the board" through effective Six Sigma project execution at the local level. Finally, the company began to look for large, global processes where improvement opportunities exist. Balancing smart local Six Sigma execution with expansive global opportunities that require the discipline of the methodologies ensures the company is always focused on the highest-impact opportunities across Intuit. "That's where we are today," says Lofgren. This current phase is really about solving for three things: (1) delivering best-we-can-be results for all stakeholders, (2) helping leaders shape mindset both strategically (how opportunities are defined) and operationally (how they execute against those opportunities), and (3) leveraging the Six Sigma and other methodologies and skills as appropriate. You'll notice that the Six Sigma methods and skills come last in this equation. It is a fundamental tenet for Intuit that having the right mindset and context to precede the methodologies and skills will deliver benefits.

One of the driving principles behind Intuit's Six Sigma efforts is the belief that three stakeholders must be incorporated into the outcomes of improvement efforts: employees, customers, and shareholders. "We must solve for all three to achieve best-we-can-be results for Intuit," says Lofgren.

Shortly after Lofgren started at Intuit, the company began examining its sales and channel marketing distribution performance and processes. The team was surprised to find that there were 64 metrics in place to gauge sales performance, one of which was the weather. The team analyzed each of those 64 metrics, eliminated those that weren't actionable, and winnowed the list down to seven. Taking an outside-in approach that starts with the customer, the team hypothesized what would be important to retailers distributing products for Intuit. They then took those six Critical to Quality requirements metrics to their top 10 customers—market leaders in software distribution such as Staples, Wal-Mart, and Costco—and asked if those metrics were their top priorities. Intuit took their input and created a closed-loop system back into the companies to let them know what action was going to be taken, what they could expect in the way of changes, what was not going to change, and why. This closed-loop system continues to be refined based on the Voice of Customer (VOC). This is another example of how Intuit has taken the mindset of outside-in thinking and operationalized it to become a part of daily life in sales and channel marketing. Creating a closed-loop process to gather and return feedback to customers promotes not only awareness, but action on the issues most concerning to customers.

As a result of improving this process, Intuit improved sales and revenue that year and won a supply chain award from one of its retail partners. The key to winning was, "We moved the dial on employee, customer, and shareholder satisfaction," says Lofgren, rather than focusing too narrowly on product performance or customers.

Intuit started with a top-down approach, looking at the organization's three core processes: (1) creating the product, (2) acquiring customers and expanding Intuit's relationship with them, and (3) servicing and fulfilling customer requests. "We then went one level down to look at the sub-processes under 'acquiring customers,'" says Lofgren, "but we did it from the customer's perspective. . . . We started with the mindset—'What is the customer experience?'"

They found the customer's experience was a bit frustrating in a couple of instances. For example, on one Intuit Web site, the team discovered that customers who wanted to report a bug in their Intuit software had to go through 26 steps to alert the company to a problem. The time and energy required of customers to make such a report was significant enough that many were giving up part of the way through the process. By reducing the bug-reporting process to four steps, instead of 26, Intuit improved the customer experience as well as the quality and quantity of information it received.

Although computer systems are easier to track and quantify than people, analyzing how systems and people interact sometimes yields important process improvements, Intuit found. In another Six Sigma initiative, Intuit decided to examine the rate at which leads were converted to customers. Looking deeper, Lofgren reports the team found, "We weren't getting the right leads to the right people at the right time." They found that 37 percent of the callers simply wanted the free product offered in the direct mailing they had received, but were not serious prospects. However, the remaining 63 percent were workable leads—"They were from customers who had high intent," says Lofgren. The root causes were around both the content of the lead and how they were prioritized. "By adding an 'intent to switch/buy' option, the ability to assign leads based on that intent and establishing sales contact and close goals enabled the sales reps to work on the highest potentials." The initial results had revenue tracking up significantly. Perhaps more importantly from the sales rep's point of view is the ability to "focus our sales energy and time on the right prospects."

Focusing on people alone—the call center sales reps—wasn't the solution, points out Lofgren. "You have to look at the system people are working within."

Although marketing is a creative process not easily mapped using Six Sigma techniques, measuring individual components is possible. The Intuit team proved that point while working to improve direct mail response rates, which were ranging from .1 to .21 percent.

Some members of the marketing team believed that introducing a fear-based message into a direct mail piece would boost response rates, such as by suggesting a dire consequence to handling payroll inaccurately in small businesses, which Intuit's software protects against. So they tested that hypothesis, along with several variations of the message and discount, and discovered that a positive, less complex offer that was needs-based, coupled with a discount, sent to a targeted customer segment produced the best response rate—more than a 100 percent improvement from baseline. Employees learned new ways to test the efficacy of their campaigns on a variety of levels and even look at interactions across different elements of a campaign. This gave marketers a new way to approach their work and determine what would resonate with customers. Additionally, customers received a customized offer of value in the direct mailer, and shareholders benefited from the additional revenue the change produced.

"Intuit frequently uses process mapping as a way to clarify discussions," says Lofgren. "At Intuit, process isn't an objective, but, rather, an enabler to achieve an objective. Processes can be helpful or negative based on how they are designed and executed. For Intuit leaders, process mapping is a way to organize around the work, which is how value is ultimately created for the customer."

Intuit also shares a passion for using root cause analysis to understand a problem at a systemic versus symptomatic level. Intuit's approach is "to ask 'why' five times to get to what's wrong with the system," she says. The classic example of this technique is the Lincoln Memorial. Years ago, Lofgren explains, the exterior of the Lincoln Memorial was being damaged—worn away—by too-frequent cleaning. First, the National Park Service tried changing cleaning agents in the hopes of reducing the damage, but when that didn't work, they started to dig deeper for the root cause of the problem. Why did the memorial need to be cleaned so frequently? Because birds were constantly leaving droppings on it. So the next solution was directed at the birds—trying to keep them away using a netting system. But when visitors complained about the netting, the team dug deeper. Why were the birds so attracted to the Lincoln Memorial? The birds came to feast on bugs—midges, actually—that flourished in the swampy area. Bug repellant did little to reduce the incidence of the insects, so the team again asked "Why?" Why were the bugs so particular to the Lincoln Memorial? Turns out, it was the bright lights shone on the property. By keeping the bright spotlights dark for an extra hour in the evening, the midge population was reduced by 90 percent, which kept the birds away, which reduced the need for excess cleaning. Asking "Why?" five times got to the root problem that was the key to process improvement.

While Intuit certainly makes use of tools and analytical processes, ensuring that its leaders had the right mindset was the company's first priority. Steve Bennett provided the inspirational vision, showing how Process Excellence could help Intuit better meet the needs of its employees, customers, and shareholders. Senior managers bought into that vision and began framing needed actions for each business unit, which then used the Six Sigma methodology applied to the highest impact opportunities.

Repeating Bennett's mantra, Lofgren says, "The business drives, the process enables."

Bank of America: Focusing on Customers and Collaboration

In 2001, Bank of America's (BofA) newly elected CEO, Ken Lewis, took a bold step. Recognizing that banking services were generally viewed as a commodity, with little to differentiate among banks, Lewis vowed BofA would break out of that mold.

That year, BofA began focusing on growing organically—that is, growing by increasing the size of its customer base while reducing operating costs through improved efficiency. A core underpinning of this strategy was customer satisfaction. In order to succeed, BofA saw it needed to keep more of its current customers while attracting new customers from competitors.

This change in strategy required an overhaul of the company's internal processes, including the adoption of Six Sigma methodologies. At Bank of America, the following steps define the Six Sigma philosophy:

- Knowing what is important to the customer
- Reducing defects
- Centering around the target
- Reducing variation

Those steps are then broken down into distinct sub-processes and analyzed using Six Sigma analytical tools. "We want to find the best way" to do something "and then make sure it's done that way every time," reports Milton Jones, Jr., BofA's quality and productivity executive in a 2004 *American Banker* article.

Beginning with the first step in the process—knowing what is important to the customer—BofA introduced the Voice of the Customer (VOC) research technique. At the time, the bank had 28 million customers, which produced almost 200 customer interactions per second, according to the ASQ article, "Driving Organic Growth at Bank of America." However, BofA found that the traditional method of segmenting its customer base by age had become ineffective. Customers of the same age could be at very different points in their life cycles, with very different banking needs. For instance, a 50-year-old woman today is just as likely to be planning for her retirement as she is to be planning for her child's future college education. Using Six Sigma analytical tools, the company identified customer needs and developed products to meet those specific needs. It also identified life triggers and sent tailored promotional materials with offers tied to those life events. The result? Delighted customers who, in turn, generated additional revenues.

In fact, BofA management learned that satisfied customers delighted with BofA are four times more likely to recommend the bank to their friends and family and three times more likely to open new accounts than customers who are just satisfied. The distinction between satisfied and delighted was an important one for the company, which proceeded to devise a plan for improving customer satisfaction across the board.

First, BofA established a customer satisfaction goal. Then it introduced a measurement process to quantify its current level of performance and committed resources to improve performance in particular areas. One of those areas was customer interaction.

To improve its customers' experience with the bank, BofA created a new associate training program called Bank of America Spirit. Its primary purpose was to help employees understand the proper way to interact with and engage customers. As a result of the training, employees in branches began greeting customers as soon as they walked in the door, quickly assessing their banking needs, rather than remaining stoically behind the teller platform.

In another initiative, BofA introduced a new online feature that allows customers to view pending transactions not yet posted to their accounts—service directed at needs customers expressed in VOC research. After that one change was made, 77 percent of BofA's online banking customers said they were more satisfied with the bank. In addition, it drove down costs by reducing use of branches. Twenty-four percent of online banking customers reduced the number of visits to branches; 38.5 percent said they would make fewer calls to the call center; and

45 percent expected to increase their use of the online banking system. That one new feature drove a 7 percent increase in online usage, an 11 percent reduction in phone calls, and a total savings of $3.9 million.

BofA worked to integrate its customer satisfaction and Six Sigma strategies, forming a continuous improvement loop that progressed from Delighting Customers to Adding Accounts to Growing Revenues to Improving Processes and Services. That strategy is working. In the first year of Six Sigma implementation, BofA generated more than $300 million in productivity gains alone, stated Ken Lewis in October of 2002. By 2004, that number had jumped to $2 billion. In addition, defects across electronic channels dropped 88 percent; errors dropped 24 percent across the board; problems taking more than one day to resolve dropped 56 percent; and the number of new checking accounts had a 174 percent year-over-year net gain.

Part of Ken Lewis's plan was to cultivate a Six Sigma culture within BofA. He started by earning his own Green Belt certification, both as an example to everyone else in the company and as a sign of his commitment to Six Sigma tools. "He wanted to send a clear message to the entire company that Six Sigma has the support of the company's most senior leadership," says Milton Jones, Jr. The company now has more than 10,000 associates trained at different levels and requires that its key vendors use Six Sigma methods.

Over the next few years, BofA customer attrition rates declined as unsatisfied customers were converted to the ranks of the satisfied and delighted customers. One of the areas the company focused its Six Sigma efforts on initially was checking account growth. Before Six Sigma was implemented, BofA had seen no growth in new checking accounts, one of its core products. Existing customers closed accounts as quickly as new accounts were opened, leading to zero growth. Teams were formed internally to address the situation, relying heavily on VOC to understand what activities would have the biggest impact. The teams honed in on reducing variations within statement rendering, deposit processing, and other high-impact processes. Within two years, the number of checking accounts was growing steadily.

But BofA also analyzed the effectiveness of its marketing efforts, including one project that verified and measured the impact of wining and dining customers. It makes sense that customers who receive special attention might turn out to be more loyal and more lucrative in the long run, but BofA set about verifying and measuring this assumption using Six Sigma. The events were upscale parties at PGA golf tournaments, which were held in several cities in 2003. BofA invited a total of 700 guests whom managers and salespeople had identified as strong BofA customers with potential for growth to these events. The bank also identified a control group of customers with a similar profile, but did not invite them to the events.

Over the course of the next 12 months, both groups were studied for any marked differences in activities. The revenue from both groups—those who had been invited to the parties and those who hadn't—both rose. But revenue from the customers who had been included in the parties rose by $30 million more than the control group. Just being invited seemed also to make a difference, as customers who had been on the guest list but couldn't attend had bigger revenue increases than the control group.

Satisfied customers do more business with BofA, and they refer other customers to the bank as well. Referrals netted 500,000 new accounts in 2002, 1.2 million in 2003, and 2 million more in 2004. Many of the referrals came from customers who rank the bank a 9 or 10 on a 10-point customer satisfaction scale, and those numbers are rising. The percentage of customers who gave BofA a 9 or 10 increased from 41 percent to 52 percent in 2004—an increase of nearly 2.5 million customers.

Although delighting its customers is BofA's primary mission, its aspirations go beyond customer satisfaction. It wants to be a true banking leader, in every sense of the word. And in 2004, it demonstrated how serious it was about that goal.

When its VOC analyses indicated customers felt the 2:00 p.m. cut-off for deposits was too restrictive, BofA took that information seriously. The Federal Reserve requires that banks credit deposits made at a branch office up until at least 2:00 p.m. on the same day, but deposits made after 2:00 p.m. are frequently rolled into the next day's deposits. Banks have historically argued that they need such a mid-afternoon cutoff in order to provide enough time for their back office operations to post deposits and payments in time to meet evening clearinghouse deadlines. But BofA decided if their customers wanted a later cutoff, they needed to find a way to provide that.

Using Six Sigma, BofA found that it was possible to improve the efficiency of its check-processing system. "The analysis technique was used to wring wasted time out of its back office sites, where the checks are handled, and to study truck routes for making deliveries more efficient," reported BofA's Christopher Marshall in an *American Banker* interview.

Beginning in February 2004, BofA began crediting customer deposits the same day, up until late afternoon, rather than the 2:00 p.m. deadline in some of its locations. Customers in eight states and Washington, D.C. could make deposits at ATM machines until 6:00 p.m. for same-day deposits, and at branches until 5:00 p.m. for same-day posting. By year-end 2004, the later cutoff was to be in place nationwide, at all BofA locations. In addition to increasing customer satisfaction, industry observers note that such a move may attract new business, especially from small business owners who dislike having to head to the bank mid-day for a deposit.

The key for BofA was: "We began to solve for a different variable," said Marshall in *American Banker*. "Instead of solving for Fed deadlines, we began solving for customer delight."

North Memorial Medical Center: Data Driven Management

"We have had a quality improvement focus for years in the emergency department (ED)," says Maribeth Woitas, RN, BSN, director of emergency services at North Memorial Medical Center in Robbinsdale, Minnesota, although the hospital's introduction to Six Sigma has only been in the last couple of years.

Viewing Six Sigma as a new approach to process improvement, in 2003 five members of the executive management team participated in Six Sigma training at the Carlson School of Management at the University of Minnesota in Minneapolis. That off-site session was followed by on-site Six Sigma training at the hospital for approximately 35 employees, including Woitas.

Taking her training back to the ED as a Six Sigma Green Belt, Woitas assembled a team to look at processes within the department where there was an opportunity for improvement. The team quickly settled on specimen collection turnaround times as the biggest department bottleneck. "Specimen collection" refers to the process of collecting blood or urine from patients for testing.

The specimen collection process, which took 46 minutes from order to result, was a source of frustration for both the emergency department and the laboratory, as is the case at many hospitals nationwide, reports Woitas. "We were frustrated by the delays that occurred while patients waited for lab test results to become available—we felt we should get better turnaround times," she says. "And the lab staff were frustrated because they believed they were doing all they could to reduce the turnaround time."

Using the seven-step process Woitas had been taught, she and her team studied the specimen collection process. "We started by looking at the process, from the time the lab test was ordered to the time the results became available to the physician," says Woitas, "and we broke it down into sub-processes."

The seven steps the team used were:

1. Establish the focus.
2. Examine the current situation.
3. Analyze the causes.
4. Act on the causes.
5. Study the results.
6. Standardize the changes.
7. Draw the conclusions.

Examine the Current Situation

Woitas and her team immediately saw that the biggest opportunity for improvement within the specimen collection process was between the time a lab test was ordered and when the specimen was actually collected. "We zeroed in on the one piece of the process that would give us the most bang for our buck," she says.

Using flowcharting and additional data collection, the team came up with a new system to bypass the delay, based on the thinking that giving the lab advance warning of a patient needing blood drawn would enable them to more evenly distribute their own workloads.

Under the new system, once a patient is in an ED bed, the admitting nurse does an assessment to determine the likelihood that a blood draw would be necessary. That assessment consists of a set of criteria, such as abdominal pain or shortness of breath in a patient over 40. If the patient meets the criteria, the nurse pages a phlebotomist from the patient's room. By the time a physician arrives and orders specific tests, the phlebotomist is already on his or her way, cutting the total time for the process by 30 minutes—from 46 minutes to 16.

Previously, the order-to-collection sub-process took a total of 22 minutes. Now, that process takes only 10 minutes.

The ED also established a goal of 12 minutes for the total time between placing a specimen collection order and the blood being drawn. At the start, 22 percent of the orders hit the target, with 78 percent taking longer than 12 minutes. But as of December 2004, the percentage of orders taking 12 minutes from start to finish is now 72 percent.

In instances where the patient does not meet the criteria, they have to wait for the physician to arrive before ordering tests. Still, the team was able to reduce this process by 5 minutes—from 46 to 41 minutes.

The team also focused on improving the percentage of times nurses used the criteria to order specimen collection in advance of the physician's seeing the patient. Increasing the number of patients with advance blood draws would reduce the amount of time spent waiting for a larger percentage of the patient population. Within a month, those percentages went from 30 percent to more than 40 percent.

Act on the Causes

The team achieved almost immediate improvement with a carefully planned and executed program to educate and encourage nurses to use the criteria. It started with the team's monitoring the percentage of times nurses were able to order specimen collection based on the criteria.

Then they examined the percentage of times each individual nurse used the criteria, generating reports showing the percentage of patients that needed blood drawn. Based on the percentage of times they used the criteria, the nurses received one of three possible letters. Those who regularly used the criteria to quickly order a specimen collection received a letter commending them for their leadership and excellent performance in that regard. Those who generally used the criteria received a letter that told them "You're doing great," and here are some ways you can further improve your performance relative to specimen collection. A third group of nurses who were inconsistent in their use of the criteria received a letter suggesting they may want to evaluate their personal practices and put a little more effort into evaluating patients for the opportunity to have an up-front specimen collected.

Woitas says there was an almost immediate positive response to the letters. They got buy-in. "We saw that people really do respond to data," she observes. "When [the nurses] saw where they were performance-wise relative to the department, they put more effort toward process improvement." It's more difficult to argue with data, she says, and keeping the analysis data-driven helped lessen emotional reactions.

As the specimen collection times have dropped, patient satisfaction has gone up, reports Woitas, because it has reduced the overall turnaround time of their visits.

Executive Management Support

Part of the ED's success can be attributed to its position as a hospital-sanctioned Six Sigma team. There are approximately 60 to 70 quality improvement projects per year at the hospital, and only about 10 percent are executive-management-sanctioned initiatives, which includes the ED's Six Sigma work.

The biggest difference between the two groups is the level of participation of the clinical improvement department. All Six Sigma initiatives hospitalwide receive access to and the support of the clinical improvement department in the hospital, but the six or seven hospital-sanctioned teams, which have the approval of senior management, work side-by-side with clinical improvement specialists to address improvement opportunities. Those teams also benefit from an internal Champion—a hospital vice president who works closely with the team to help obtain needed resources.

Although hospital-sanctioned initiatives have advantages over smaller projects, John DeVries, manager, improvement systems for North Memorial says, "Our organization values improvement initiatives and encourages individual department initiatives….The greatest opportunity for success in individual department initiatives is to be sure and select a project that is within the scope of their control."

Part Four

Bringing Two Worlds Together: Manager Meets Black Belt

Chapter 12

Management Perceptions of Six Sigma

Hear the other side.

—Saint Augustine

If you're reading this book, I'm guessing that you fall into one of these categories:

1. Functional manager working at a company that has not committed to Six Sigma
2. Functional manager working at a company that is committed to Six Sigma
3. Six Sigma or quality management professional interested in the topic

Regardless of your category, you should be concerned about what happens when Six Sigma professionals come together with functional management to form a team responsible to carry out a Six Sigma project. As managers, implementing your own Six Sigma program within your scope of responsibility will prepare you for a companywide Six Sigma commitment when that time comes. You will be far ahead of your peers in understanding how to work with Six Sigma professionals to accomplish the project goals. It may be that you were involved in convincing senior management to commit to Six Sigma; either way, you and your personal organization will be in an excellent position to accept the culture change that will face the rest of the company. The odds are that you will have laid valuable groundwork with your internal suppliers and customers. If you're a manager who wishes to implement your own Six Sigma program, but you also have a companywide commitment to Six Sigma, you are clearly at an advantage in that you have a Six Sigma support system available to you on site.

Most companies that have traditional Six Sigma programs are selective about what projects they choose to take on. You may or may not have served on a Six Sigma project team yet. Depending on your scope of responsibility within the company, most likely, you will still want to put your own program in place. Remember, it's all about how you choose to manage your responsibilities! If you are a Six Sigma professional and you care about the long-term possibilities for Six Sigma, you should be interested in understanding the perceptions that functional managers have about the important work that you're doing.

In her article, "High-Performance Teams and Their Impact on Organizations," Mary Ellen Collins suggests that high-performance teams exhibit behaviors similar to those of a newly converted member of a religion or an elite club. Many Six Sigma professionals exhibit this kind of dedication and passion, which is fantastic! However, if the long-term goal of the Six Sigma or quality management professional is to create companywide and industrywide changes in how we manage our businesses, functional management needs to understand what drives that passion. They also need to join the religion of Six Sigma!

Committing to Six Sigma

In companies that have committed to using a comprehensive Six Sigma approach, Six Sigma professionals at all levels must interact with various levels of functional management to accomplish the goals of the project team. It's critical that teams comprised of these two groups function at high performance levels because they must work together to achieve the best outcome. In addition to achieving the project team goals, Six Sigma professionals should have an additional goal of infusing quality concepts and philosophies into the lifeblood of the organizations they support.

What happens within the Six Sigma project team is critical to the long-term acceptance of Six Sigma concepts by functional managers. Throughout my experience as both a functional manager and a quality management professional in several major pharmaceutical companies, my educational journey, and my experiences attending and speaking at various Six Sigma- and quality management-related conferences, I have observed a common gap when it comes to post-project perceptions of Six Sigma. In conjunction with the Department of Engineering and Technology Management at Polytechnic State University in Marietta, Georgia, I set out to explore the perceptions of functional management, as well as the Six Sigma/quality professionals' level of understanding about those perceptions. To do this, the following problem statement was developed:

"What are the most common, avoidable reasons why project teams, composed of Six Sigma/quality professionals and functional managers, fail to function at high performance levels and what specific actions can Six Sigma professionals take to improve success rates?"

The peer-reviewed Six Sigma and quality management literature does not adequately address this topic. Therefore, survey and interview data were gathered to explore the question. High-level conclusions from an independent survey, a recent private survey from a major pharmaceutical company, and interview data show statistical differences between the views of Six Sigma professionals and functional management who have worked together on project teams.

Depending on the parent company, the Six Sigma organization can be structured in various ways, including the following most common scenarios:

- Six Sigma professionals report directly into the functional organization. High-performing individuals are selected to attend Black Belt training and then manage projects within their function. These Six Sigma professionals work within a specific function and often have experience in that functional discipline or develop appropriate expertise. They are reliant on their functional counterparts to implement Six Sigma concepts into the workflow or management system.

Or

- Six Sigma professionals report into a separate organization such as Quality Assurance, Quality Systems, Process Excellence, etc. These Six Sigma professionals must work closely with functional management on assigned Six Sigma or quality projects. They may or may not have any operational experience in the functional discipline, and, therefore, are reliant on the process owners and other functional experts to apply Six Sigma to the operation as well as into the workflow or management system.

Six Sigma professionals, regardless of how they are organized within the company, should manage the long-term impact on the functional managers involved in the current project or initiative. Six Sigma professionals know that high-level support is absolutely critical for implementation of Six Sigma throughout the company; however, they should also know that *quality, efficiency, and a desire to impact the bottom line* should not be a program or special initiative. These are excellent business practices and, therefore, the responsibility of each manager. Results in these areas are best achieved when supported by all levels of management and embraced by each person producing a deliverable within the organization. Acknowledgment of the long-term goal of achieving positive perceptions (particularly after the project ends) on the part of functional managers calls for an expanded Six Sigma definition of the high-performance team.

Creating High-Performance Teams

A concise definition of a high-performance team is difficult to find in the peer-reviewed literature. Instead there are many detailed explanations available. The general components are:

- Shared vision
- Clear goals with associated timelines
- Excellent communication
- Consistent checks to ensure quality of work
- Involvement of entire team
- Self-direction
- Celebration of success

A suggested additional component for a Six Sigma high-performance team that involves both Six Sigma professionals and functional management is:

- Achievement of long-term positive Six Sigma impact on the functional management

Given a predefined definition of a high-performance team that includes the added component above, data obtained via an extensive literature search and an independent survey will show the most common, avoidable reasons why project teams, composed of both groups fail to function at high-performance levels. A survey was distributed to both groups and the data analyzed independently to determine if each group attributes the same reasons to team failure. At the onset of the study, it was anticipated that the most common reasons would be related to communication and the establishment and acceptance of goals driven by common motivating factors—and indeed, this was the case.

The outcome of this research benefits Six Sigma professionals by providing a clearer understanding of project team success from the functional manager's point of view. Six Sigma professionals have learned about the key elements of successful teams and have set out to implement those key elements in cross-functional teams. They have also focused on the bottom line success of individual projects. They have applied Six Sigma tools to projects and, in some (if not most) cases, have seen fantastic bottom-line success. However, looking back to the underlying philosophy that quality, efficiency, and cost reductions shouldn't be a special project, initiative, or program, this research suggests that Six Sigma professionals should ask themselves whether the Six Sigma tools and concepts they are advocating have really been integrated into the mainstream business philosophies of the organization. Is this happening? The research delved into this question through analysis of survey and interview data coupled with the current literature on this and related topics to flesh out project success and failure from two points of view: the Six Sigma/quality professional and the functional manager. The data and results were analyzed to determine if a new approach would benefit Six Sigma professionals in accomplishing their initial, underlying resolve to infuse the concepts they advocate into the day-to-day culture of their companies.

Surprisingly, the peer-reviewed literature does not adequately address this topic. There were only a few recent articles that discuss reasons for Six Sigma project team failure. These articles focus on project failure as an outcome of team failure rather than on the specific team interactions and communication that may or may not contribute to the project outcome. They do not provide research-based conclusions about the dynamics of Six Sigma teams comprised of Six Sigma professionals and functional management. There is a tremendous amount of literature on Six Sigma. However, most of it focuses on the tools and techniques of Six Sigma and success stories of Six Sigma teams. Because of the lack of specific information on the topic in the peer-reviewed literature, a search was performed using a popular Internet search program. A few additional non-peer-reviewed articles were found that specified distinct reasons for team failure; however, they are not based on standard research methodology. Instead they are heavily based on the author's opinion from career experience, or other illusive sources. However, these articles will also be discussed. In general, the literature search suggested that while there are many people who have strong opinions about the dynamics of Six Sigma project teams and the factors that lead to failure, research data to support these ideas has not been provided, nor has it been published in the peer-reviewed literature.

Many general articles on high-performance teams were found in the literature. In narrowing down the search to include literature on high-performance teams related to quality, several stood out. In her article, "The Collaborative Experience," Joni Daniels says that professional teams in the workplace can be derailed by the history and past experiences of the members, a leader whose style doesn't fit, or an organizational culture that rewards individual success rather than team success. The predictable phases of team formation—forming, storming, norming, and performing—have been well established in the literature. Daniel's article focuses on how leadership impacts the team's ability to move through these stages effectively and efficiently. She proposes that a well-trained leader is an essential ingredient for team success. According to Daniels, the difference between a group, a team, and a high-performing work team rests with the chemistry between the members and the leader. In contrast to Daniel's opinion, in his article, "High-Performance Teams: Lessons from the Pygmies," Manfred De Vries suggests that members of a team should subscribe to "distributed" leadership in order to reach high performance. De Vries says that in taking a close look at high-performance organizations, you will find an attitude of distributed leadership at its core. His examples are leaders who encourage full participation and are willing to share goals. They avoid secrecy at all costs. They treat members of the teams with respect, listen to feedback, and ask questions, address problems, and display tolerance and flexibility. He goes on to list other characteristics of leaders who have a "distributed leadership" approach. Interestingly, he lists many of the same qualities that Daniels puts forth and does not provide highly relevant examples of team success based on "distributed" leadership. Instead, team success appears to hinge on an excellent leader. In general, both of the articles discussed above and a third article titled, "High-Performance Teams and Their Impact on Organizations," by Mary Ellen Collins suggest similar traits for high-performance teams. A summary of these is provided below:

- Sharing a strong common goal and purpose based on shared values and beliefs
- Mutual accountability, respect, and trust
- Complementary skills
- Highly supportive and communicative members
- Excellent leadership

Of course, Mary Ellen Collins takes these traits a step further to suggest that high-performance teams exhibit behaviors similar to those of a newly converted member of a religion or an elite club.

Does ROI Equal Success?

In moving beyond a general definition of the high-performance team and considering the lack of peer-reviewed literature surrounding Six Sigma project teams and their failure to reach high-performance levels, it is interesting to note that none of the three articles on high-performance teams spoke of monetary gain, return on investment (ROI), or actual achievement of the shared team goal. It can be assumed that either the team goal is achieved, or that high-performance team qualities contribute to a broader organizational cultural gain than just meeting the goal at hand. In his article, "Understanding Six Sigma Deployment Failures," Mike Carnell, coauthor of several Six Sigma books including *Leaning into Six Sigma*, defines the term *failure* as anything that does not deliver the ROI required by the company or any other investment.

At its most basic definition, Six Sigma is a quality improvement approach that focuses on lowering defects in order to achieve fantastic levels of quality evidenced by cost savings. These savings are what Six Sigma professionals and other supporters suggest functional management use to engage senior management in the philosophy. Senior management support is needed to successfully deploy Six Sigma on a broad-based organizational level. However, Carnell's article speaks of deployment not at the level of an overarching organizational spread, but rather at the project level. He states that Six Sigma consultants typically define successful deployment as one that provides an acceptable ROI and leaves a stand-alone program (not requiring further assistance from outside resources). This definition suggests that he is referring to an organizational deployment, but the list of reasons for failure that he includes in the article are specifically related to project team performance and Six Sigma professional and functional management failures, which suggests that failures of the teams responsible for accomplishing the goals of Six Sigma can lead to the overall failure of any broad organizational deployment that serves as the ultimate goal. Carnell provides a detailed list of reasons for failure, which appears to be based on his consulting experience, which is no doubt a reliable indication of top reasons. The list provides excellent insight into potential reasons for failure for which both Six Sigma professionals and functional management are responsible. A few of these examples are provided here.

Failures Attributed to Six Sigma Professionals

- Treating the project as an academic exercise
- Failing to appreciate the complexity of dealing with people
- Not transferring ownership of the solution to the team as the project progresses (the solution becomes personality dependent)
- Spending too much time on the computer and not enough time in the process
- Presenting results as if this were a science project—using things such as ANOVA tables to convey results
- Creating an exclusive attitude around the program
- Taking credit for work accomplished by another initiative or an ongoing project

Failures Attributed to Functional Management

- No concept of customer expectations
- Lack of alignment (horizontal or vertical)
- Trying to change the organization without a detailed change process
- Having metrics in place, but no feedback (or limited feedback)
- A project selection process that does not identify projects related to business objectives
- Middle management that operates on its own agenda (feels support is optional)
- No accountability

- No buy-in at the process-owner level
- Process owner who believes he or she has the option to not buy-in

In summary, the peer-reviewed literature does not fully address this topic, but does address the general topic of team success and high-performance team criteria. Internet sources can provide additional information on Six Sigma project teams, including proposed reasons for failure on the part of both Six Sigma professionals and functional management, primarily based on the experience of consultants rather than standard research methodologies.

Survey of Quality Management Professionals and Functional Management

In conjunction with Southern Polytechnic State University, Department of Engineering and Technology Management, a survey was designed and administered to obtain data from both Six Sigma/quality professionals and functional managers. The responders, who have served on a least one project team that included both groups, were asked to designate their roles, as well as respond to the following statements using a five-point Likert scale for ease of analysis (strongly disagree, disagree, not sure, agree, and strongly agree):

- Six Sigma is a set of tools used for quality improvement efforts.
- Six Sigma is a management philosophy.
- Six Sigma teams in which I have participated have been high-performance teams.
- Six Sigma professionals have an appropriate respect for the expertise of functional managers.
- Functional managers have an appropriate respect for the expertise of Six Sigma professionals.
- Six Sigma professionals have a realistic understanding of how busy functional managers stay in order to meet day-to-day goals and objectives.
- The functional managers and the Six Sigma professionals in the team shared a strong common vision.
- Six Sigma professionals lack functional expertise.
- Functional managers lack commitment to Six Sigma projects or initiatives.
- Too many requirements are imposed on functional managers by Six Sigma professionals given their busy schedules.
- Functional managers did not understand the Six Sigma philosophy.
- There was a lack of senior management support for the project.

- Timelines established by functional managers were realistic.
- Timelines established by Six Sigma professionals were realistic.
- There was excellent team leadership.
- Functional managers placed high priority on the Six Sigma-related tasks/tools.
- Six Sigma professionals treated the project as an academic exercise.
- Six Sigma professionals appreciated the complexity of dealing with people.
- Six Sigma professionals transferred ownership of the solution to the team as the project progressed.
- Six Sigma professionals created an exclusive attitude around the project.
- Functional management did not care enough about the project.
- The Six Sigma training provided to functional managers on the team was adequate.
- Quality of communication between the Six Sigma professionals and the functional managers contributed to the success of the project.

The statements were created based on the standard and expanded definition for high-performance team, items from the literature research, and author observation. The survey was distributed to a subset of Johnson & Johnson (J&J) employees. The J&J employees chosen were comprised of an even split between Six Sigma/quality professionals and functional management. In addition, to gain a broader perspective, the survey was distributed to a subset of the Southern Polytechnic State University students enrolled in the Quality Assurance Master's Degree program available through the Department of Engineering and Technology Management. The majority of the students are full-time employees either in Six Sigma/quality-related or functional management positions. Finally, the survey was distributed to a subset of the American Society for Quality (ASQ) members through direct distribution to four chapters of the organization: Atlanta, Georgia; Raleigh, North Carolina; Charlotte, North Carolina; and Eastern Tennessee.

Analysis of the Independent Survey

The response rate fell just above 40 percent, which is considered an excellent outcome. Of the surveys returned, 56.1 percent were from Quality Management professionals and 43.9 percent were from functional management, which provided a fairly even split in the data for analysis purposes. Using the Likert-scale ratings, statistical analysis was performed for each survey question. The first three survey questions related to the respondents' understanding of Six Sigma and whether the Six Sigma teams in which they had participated were high-performance teams.

Not surprisingly, 92.2 percent of the Six Sigma/quality management profession-als and 100 percent of the functional management either agreed or strongly agreed that Six Sigma is a set of tools used for quality improvement efforts. When asked if they agreed that Six Sigma is a management philosophy, 75.0 percent of Six Sigma/quality management professionals versus 64.0 percent of the functional management agreed or strongly agreed. Of the respondents who agreed or strongly agreed that their teams had functioned at high performance, 66.3 percent were Six Sigma/quality professionals and 33.7 percent were func-tional management. Of the Six Sigma/quality professionals who responded to the survey, 86 percent agreed or strongly agreed, but only 56 percent of func-tional management agreed or strongly agreed. These results were all statistically significant.

Other key results from the survey were:

- 100 percent of Six Sigma/quality professionals agreed or strongly agreed that Six Sigma professionals have an appropriate respect for the expertise of functional managers versus 72 percent of functional management.
- Only 12.5 percent of the Six Sigma/quality professionals agreed or strong-ly agreed that Six Sigma professionals lack functional expertise versus 32.0 percent of functional management.
- A higher percentage of Six Sigma/quality professionals (92.1 percent versus 68.0 percent) felt that timelines established by them were realistic, but a higher percentage of functional managers felt that timelines established by functional managers were realistic (84.0 percent versus 62.5 percent).
- Only 3.1 percent of Six Sigma/quality professionals felt that they treated projects as an academic exercise versus 30 percent of functional manage-ment.
- Only 1.6 percent of Six Sigma/quality professionals agreed that they creat-ed an exclusive attitude versus 34 percent of functional managers.
- 39.1 percent of Six Sigma/quality professionals felt that functional man-agers did not care enough about the project, whereas only 12 percent of the functional managers agreed or strongly agreed.
- Of the respondents, only 24 percent were either not sure, disagreed, or strongly disagreed that the Six Sigma teams in which they had participated were high performing. Interestingly, 73 percent of the functional managers who felt that their teams were not high-performing teams disagreed that they were provided adequate training at project start. Also, 79 percent of the functional managers who agreed that the Six Sigma professionals creat-ed an exclusive attitude around the project did not believe their team was high performing.

- The majority of the respondents (92.1 percent), both Six Sigma/quality professionals and functional management (92.2 percent and 92.0 percent, respectively—no statistical significant difference) agreed or strongly agreed that quality of communication between the two groups contributed to the success of the project.

When you consider J&J employees who function within the bounds of the J&J Credo and its long-standing commitment to quality, the types of students who would enroll in a Master's program in Quality Assurance, and the types of people who would be interested in joining the ASQ, one could suspect that the differences between Six Sigma professionals and functional management would be even more divergent if the survey were distributed more widely in the industries where Six Sigma is being advocated.

The independent survey data shows that there are statistically significant differences between post-project perceptions of the Six Sigma/quality professionals and the functional managers serving on the teams. These differences may be hindering Six Sigma professionals from infusing long-term quality philosophies into the managers' world post-project. Informal interviews were also conducted to gain insight into some of the anecdotal reasons for the differing perceptions. Interviewees were selected from the independent survey respondent pool. During the interviews, attitudes that mirror the survey data were observed. Following are a few specific anecdotal comments that were shared:

- "We had a critical project meeting in which there were about seven Six Sigma professionals and about eight functional managers. The room was a bit too small and all the Six Sigma professionals sat around the conference table while the key functional managers had to go get chairs. Everyone was appalled, because it's our project. It's our work and they should be facilitating." —Operations Director
- "It's the people factor that kills us—getting people to understand what we're trying to accomplish."—Six Sigma Black Belt
- "The Black Belt kept sending me new charts and sheets to fill out every day! It was driving me nuts because I have so much to do. I'm committed to the project but I can't spend that much time creating tables and sheets that, in my opinion, serve to help her better understand my work."—Functional Manager

Process Excellence (PE) Survey Results

The response rate for the PE survey was 60 percent, also an excellent return. The breakdown of respondents between PE professionals and functional management was not available, nor were the detailed results. However, the high-level summary results available appear to support the independent survey data. Nearly all of the functional management respondents (88 percent) agreed that PE could provide significant value for their business; however, only 50 percent were satisfied with the actual progress they are making with PE. The majority of functional management surveyed had a favorable perception of each of the elements of PE; there were, however, differences among the elements with improvement methodologies and Dashboards being the most highly valued and assessment less valued. Interestingly, the PE staff surveyed responded that they need more support from the functional management, as well as from the corporate-level PE groups while the functional management surveyed indicated that they need more support from their PE staff. The survey results also highlight that while many people are positive about the projects, they did not feel that enough progress had been made or that each group was best supporting the other. This suggests a breakdown in understanding the needs of each group.

The Bottom Line

- The topic of this research is not adequately addressed in the peer-reviewed literature.
- The literature does not provide research-based conclusions about the dynamics of project teams comprised of Six Sigma professionals and functional management.
- In an independent survey, both Six Sigma/quality professionals and functional management agreed that Six Sigma is a set of tools used for quality management efforts, but there was a statistically significant difference in the belief that Six Sigma is a management philosophy.
- In the survey, there were statistically significant differences in the level of respect each group had for the other's expertise in the functional area and/or the perception of that respect.
- There were also statistically significant differences in opinions about the timelines being established by each group.
- Other areas where opinions strongly differed were related to Six Sigma/quality professionals treating projects as academic exercises and having an exclusive attitude.
- A large percentage of respondents who were either unsure or did not believe their project team was high performing also believed that they were not provided adequate training at project start and felt that the Six Sigma professionals created an exclusive attitude around the project.

- Both groups agreed that the quality of communication between the two groups contributed to project success.
- Both interview data and high-level results of a recent J&J survey of Process Excellence professionals and functional management support the project findings.

Chapter 13

Creating a New Breed of Six Sigma Leaders

A leader is best when people barely know he exists. Not so good when people obey and acclaim him. Worse when they despise him. But of a good leader who talks little when his work is done, his aim fulfilled, they will say, "We did it ourselves."

—Lao-tzu, c. 550 B.C.

Functional managers and Six Sigma professionals can both aspire to the good leadership described by Lao-tzu. Functional managers can lead Six Sigma projects and teams by creating a management framework strongly supported by a collaborative spirit. Six Sigma professionals can infuse the underlying concepts of Six Sigma into the business philosophies of all management layers. There are some companies with more mature Six Sigma programs that require Green Belt training for all employees or for all managers. However, the underlying concepts of Six Sigma can and should be built into required management training at all companies—business excellence training that incorporates these concepts with the realities of day-to-day management.

In this book, managers have learned some of the basic principles that support the current quality management systems and philosophies. The United States Congress supports these concepts through their Malcolm Baldrige Award program. The U.S. Congress has included the key concepts of Six Sigma within their definition and recognition of business excellence. The International Standards Organization (ISO), a global institute that creates and agrees upon common principles, also includes these underlying concepts. With the advent of Six Sigma, a specific methodology and organizational structure (e.g., Champions, Master Black Belts, Black Belts, Green Belts) by which to use these basic concepts was made available. It has become evident through published successes and company savings that this standardized approach can be used across functions and industries. Until now, managers have played the roles of process owners, supporting team members, or subject matter experts in the game of Six Sigma. Depending on the company, they have been provided various degrees of training prior to project start. Because of the strong high-level support needed to make Six Sigma work at a company-wide level, many times managers and their employees have been told that the project is high priority by their senior management. In many, if not most, cases they have played their roles well, supporting the projects. But have they gained a true appreciation for Six Sigma and its concepts? Have they been able to walk away from the project and implement some of the same concepts and strategies within their own work? Have they wanted to?

As a quality management professional, I believe the longest-term goal of all our efforts should be to change culture and instill a belief in the organization that quality management is simply good management—a component of business excellence. With this as our goal, why would we not want to infuse our belief in these principles and methodologies into all layers of management?

This book provided a high-level overview of some of the most straightforward Six Sigma tools. Managers were provided with some food for thought regarding why implementation of the underlying concepts and methodology of Six Sigma into their day-to-day operations makes good business and personal sense. A management framework centered on the key concepts, using the J&J Credo as an example, was encouraged as a way to build the concepts into the manager's day-by-day thinking, decision making, and execution. Sharing the framework with staff was shown as a requirement for infusing the concepts into their hearts and minds to move forward as a true team and begin to create a culture for their own personal organization. Showing managers at all levels that, no matter what the scope or size of their organizations, they are the leaders is *key* to creating a culture that is leading somewhere. An important part of being a leader is leading toward something rather than simply practicing routine management. Routine management helps to "manage things" so that the status quo is maintained. Leadership is about inspiring people, building teams, taking an organization from point A to point B, and, as we heard from Lao-tzu, somehow instilling in each individual a sense of accomplishment and ownership.

Managers were ushered through the DMAIC method first through specific examples of how each of the key concepts: process focus, customer focus and collaboration, and data driven management could be applied within their scope of work, regardless of size. They were then provided with a specific strategy to plan for quality that centered on the DMAIC method. Explaining how each of the underlying concepts can impact them and their teams provides a unique understanding of why these concepts are good business practices. Following up with how managers specifically fit into the DMAIC methodology provided them with an appreciation of how Six Sigma ties it all together. Managers were challenged to be creative along the way and to question each and every task, activity, and document they create to ensure that it is value-added given the time it would take to complete. With that said, they were shown examples of how value can be added.

Once managers were comfortable with how they might be able to apply Six Sigma in their own work, they were provided more in-depth information about how traditional Six Sigma programs work, the players involved, and some of the important attributes needed to successfully fulfill the key roles. A brief history of Six Sigma was provided as well as a list of some of the companies that use Six Sigma. By seeing all the companies that have Six Sigma programs in place and understanding that Six Sigma expertise has all but become a career path in industry, managers could hopefully appreciate that knowing more about Six Sigma and incorporating it into their management styles, choices, and techniques could only be a plus! Case studies from manufacturing and nonmanufacturing companies were provided in an effort to inspire thought about how the methods, techniques, tools, strategies, and methodology used by these companies could also be used in a manager's own work to meet specific goals and drive culture.

Given the challenge of instilling long-term acceptance of the underlying concepts of Six Sigma into managers at all levels within the organization, there may be an advantage to exploring alternative ways to infuse these concepts into the very heart of our organizations. The need to do so may be hard to understand, considering all the successes we've heard and read about, particularly those presented in Chapters 10 and 11 of this book. It's just strange that with all the successes, I still hear grumbling before or after meetings, while having business dinners, or when networking with people from other companies with a traditional commitment to Six Sigma. This always occurs when guards are down and everyone's relaxed and feeling fine. There seems to be an undercurrent of concern from functional management inside traditional Six Sigma organizations as to the long-term value and relevance of Six Sigma to their day-to-day issues, schedules, and goals. *That is what this book is all about.* Middle management cannot deny the successes of Six Sigma; many of us are fascinated by it. But it's still a bit beyond our reach, a methodology handed down by company edict. Some are feeling that they must fit the round job they do into a square method, that the high-level support that is so desperately needed sometimes feels like bureaucracy, even in the DMAIC cycle.

But it doesn't have to be this way. Some would describe Six Sigma as a revolution, but the revolution has yet to begin.

I love Six Sigma. Since I first learned about it as a young manager, I have been fascinated by its ability to provide a framework for managing my responsibilities.

At the time, I could not gain support to attend the training, which was 10 times more expensive at the time, so I began planning to earn a Master's Degree in Quality Systems via the tuition reimbursement program easily available to me. Its underlying concepts continue to support my own personal business principles and I still can't quite figure out why it's call quality management and not just management. It involves people, process, money, and all the elements of management. It makes common sense. It provides a strategy for moving forward, for reaching high goals and bringing people and ideas together. I *am* like a member of new religion as Mary Collins described in her article, but I recognize that to give longevity to the movement, it has to become "the way we do business" rather than "the way we do Six Sigma."

Six Sigma professionals must practice what they preach (e.g., customer focus, collaboration, innovation, etc.) and show functional management that Six Sigma is for them, too. Managers can own its concepts and apply its strategy within their own scope. They can intertwine it into their business practices and management styles. Then, when presented with Six Sigma projects that span departments, business units and, in the case of J&J or GE, companies, they will be prepared to contribute and, even more importantly, to become the executive leaders of the future—those who lend their strong support to keeping Six Sigma alive.

According to Paul Keller, author of *Six Sigma Demystified*, "There are plenty of people trying to implement a Six Sigma approach on their own, and they could obviously use some guidance." He agrees that process focus, customer focus, collaboration, data driven management, and strategic planning for quality are all good business practices. Keller has also seen positive results from middle managers who have implemented the underlying concepts of Six Sigma within their own scope of responsibility, notably in pilot studies in autonomous companies' units. These initial successes were often used to prove the worth of the program to upper management. Keller and I agree that the goal should ultimately be to get others "on board" by example. According to Keller, "The use of data to drive decision making will be a key contribution of this initial effort." For me, this means getting your colleagues as well as your senior management on board. Now that wide acceptance of Six Sigma in industry has paved the way, this is where the revolution begins. It begins in the trenches, not in the boardroom. Revolutions aren't easy to start or finish, but they are worth the effort; they are the stuff of true cultural transformation—even beyond one company or one industry.

Another noteworthy figure in the world of Six Sigma and the author of numerous Six Sigma books, George Eckes, also agrees that the concepts discussed in this book are key to making Six Sigma a true cultural phenomenon and not just a money-making project. According to Eckes, most organizations are highly inefficient and ineffective because they're not process focused. He says, "In order to become a good, effective organization, you must be customer- and process-focused." This holds true for both your overall organization or company and your own personal organization, whether you run the human resources department, a pharmacovigilance unit, an automotive repair shop, or a Six Sigma organization within GE, J&J, or Toyota. Eckes provided the following advantages for middle management to have a process, customer, and collaborative focus:

- By definition, functional boundaries build inefficiency and ineffectiveness. By being more process- and customer-focused, middle managers can begin to lay the foundation for improved efficiency and effectiveness, which helps the company become more profitable and achieve business objectives.
- By achieving those objectives, the middle manager can become a star in and out of the company, creating new promotion and career opportunities.

As a result of the research done in conjunction with Southern Polytechnic State University, it was concluded that Six Sigma professionals might wish to consider taking the following actions or approaches in their interactions with functional management when serving on traditional Six Sigma teams together:

- Provide as much training as possible for functional management at project start.
- Improve overall customer service attitude and/or approach toward the functional management; develop strong facilitation skills, and allow functional management to own projects.
- Spend more up-front time on developing the expectations of each group regarding the roles and responsibilities within the team.
- Explore ways to improve communicating a high respect for the expertise of functional managers as well as an understanding of their day-to-day challenges.

Of course, Six Sigma professionals are excited about their work. They are learning new things, putting them into practice, and seeing results. Beyond the recommendations above, if the Six Sigma philosophy is perpetuated throughout the organization in a way that speaks more personally to managers, Six Sigma professionals will reap the rewards. If functional managers interested in Six Sigma are provided a strategy to incorporate the underlying concepts and methodologies into their own scope of responsibility and if Six Sigma professionals can create new and innovate ways to infuse long-term acceptance of the concepts into the management layer, all will benefit. This is a win-win scenario because, as the two groups converge, they will have a more natural common interest in the projects and project activities presented.

Six Sigma professionals are already aware of the tremendous impact of change within organizations. Change management has become a science. This will continue to be critical for all forms of Six Sigma. Why not spend some time and effort getting into the trenches to understand how middle management can "buy-in" to Six Sigma far beyond supporting the project at hand? Why not teach them the underlying concepts in ways that specifically apply to their work? Think of the possibilities that could result from a combination of Six Sigma from the top down and Six Sigma from the bottom up. What about Six Sigma from the outside in (Black Belts and consultants driving projects) and Six Sigma from the inside out (functional management driving projects)? Perhaps it makes you nervous—that's just a response to change.

In most cases, functional managers are never going to be statistical whizzes. They are not going to spend hours using complex statistical methods to support their projects, creating beautiful detailed visuals of their processes, highly complex control charts, and so on. In many cases, this would neither be an efficient use of the manager's time, nor would it be needed when tackling their internally owned processes. They need methods and tools that are easy, straightforward, and beneficial on the spot. It's not that they lack the brainpower to learn how to do all this, it's just that they have other priorities, and rightly so. They often have many direct and indirect reports knocking at the door throughout the day. They have fixed, routine deliverables to produce that must continue as processes are questioned and improved. They have internal and/or external suppliers and customers calling, inviting them to meetings, etc. The critical priorities they *do* share with Six Sigma professionals are the desire to see results, to improve, to move the business forward, and to impact the organization in a positive way. If Six Sigma professionals can tap into this common ground by inspiring functional management and providing both business excellence training and straightforward tools and methods for incorporating the underlying concepts of Six Sigma into their worlds, many of the hidden inefficiencies within organizations that, on their own, may not get the attention of the CEO but collectively impact the bottom line would be eliminated.

Through the Johnson & Johnson Credo values, the company serves as a leader in promoting a management framework intended to drive business decisions and practices. The company also challenges each employee to stand for something, putting customers at the forefront at all times, and focusing on quality. Its process excellence program is supported by Six Sigma methodology and reaches across functions and J&J companies. Years ago, Robert W. Johnson chose the underlying concepts of Six Sigma when he wrote the famous Credo. He saw these concepts as the basis for business excellence. Through adherence to a Credo that began as a personal management framework, Johnson & Johnson has become one of the most successful companies in history. There must be something to it.

Let us go forward in creating a new breed of Six Sigma leaders—leaders that rise from the ranks of management and Six Sigma professionals who embrace the notion that the underlying quality management concepts of Six Sigma are the cornerstones of business excellence, not just the cornerstones of Six Sigma. Let's find a way to give Six Sigma to the people who own the processes.

As managers, let us rise to the challenge of thinking outside the Six Sigma box to embrace its concepts and methodologies as our own and show our senior management that we own something, we lead something, and we are headed in the direction of change. On our own, we can at the very least apply Six Sigma to our own scope of work. We can build culture within our personal organizations. We can strategize to bring quality and an impact to the bottom line into our day-to-day goals. And then, as we move up within our organizations, we can truly understand the importance of Six Sigma. We can evolve into the Executive Leaders and Six Sigma Champions of tomorrow.

Sources

Armstrong, Ronald, "Creating a Team-Based High-Performance Workplace," 2005, http://rvarmstrong.com/CreatingTeamBarsedWorkplaceArticle.htm.

Brue, Greg, *Six Sigma for Managers*, New York: McGraw-Hill, 2002.

Carnell, Mike, "Understanding Six Sigma Deployment Failures," 2005, http://www.isixsigma.com/library/content/c020916a.asp.

Collins, Mary Ellen, "High-Performance Teams and Their Impact on Organizations," *Journal for Quality & Participation*, 18, 7, 1995, 24–27.

De Feo, Joseph and William W. Barnard, *Juran Institute's Six Sigma Breakthrough and Beyond*, New York: McGraw-Hill, 2004.

De Vries, M. and F. R. Kets, "High-Performance Teams: Lessons from the Pygmies," *Organizational Dynamics*, 27, 3, 66–78.

Eckes, George, *Six Sigma for Everyone*, New York: John Wiley & Sons, 2003.

Federico, Mary, "The Role of Human Resources (HR) in Six Sigma," 2005, http://isixsigma.com/library/content/c030414a.sap.

Gilbert, Bob, "Sick Sigma," 2005, http://www.contextmag.com/archive/200208/Feature 2SickSigma.asp.

Gitlow, Howard, *Quality Management Systems: A Practical Guide*, Boca Raton, Fla.: St. Lucie Press, 2001.

Goldstein, Mark, "Six Sigma Program Success Factors," *Six Sigma Forum Magazine*, 1, 2001, 1.

Gupta, Praveen, *Six Sigma Business Scorecard*, New York: McGraw-Hill, 2004.

Harrington, James, *ISO 9000 and Beyond*, New York: McGraw-Hill, 1997.

ISO 9000, International Standard: Quality Management Systems— Fundamentals and Vocabulary, 2000.

Joiner, Brian, "Total Quality Leadership vs. Management by Results," 2005, http://deming.eng.clemson.edu/pub/den/files/tql.txt.

Juran, Joseph and A. Blanton Godfrey, *Juran's Quality Handbook*, Fifth Edition, New York: McGraw-Hill, 1999.

Lamprecht, James, *Quality and Power in the Supply Chain*, Boston: Butterworth-Heinemann, 2000.

Morris, D. S. and R. H. Haigh, et al., "How to Stop Quality Improvement Teams from Quitting," *Total Quality Management*, 5, 1994, 4.

Nardi, Peter M., *Doing Survey Research: A Guide to Quantitative Methods*, Boston: Pearson Education, 2003.

National Institute of Standards and Technology, 2005, www.nist.gov.

Nickols, Fred, "Change Management 101," 2005, http://home.att.net/~nickols/change.htm.

Pande, Peter S., Robert Neuman, and Roland Cavanagh, *The Six Sigma Way: How GE, Motorola, and Other Top Companies Are Honing Their Perspective*, New York: McGraw-Hill, 2000.

Pande, Peter S. and Larry Holpp, *What Is Six Sigma?*, New York: McGraw-Hill, 2002.

Pande, Peter S., Robert Neuman, and Roland Cavanagh, *The Six Sigma Way: Team Fieldbook*, New York: McGraw-Hill, 2002.

Parsowith, B. Scott, *Fundamentals of Quality Auditing*, Milwaukee: Quality Press, 1995.

Pyzdek, Thomas, "Why Six Sigma Is Not TQM," 2005, http://www.pyzdek.com/six_sigma-vs_tqm.htm.

Slater, Robert, *Jack Welch and the GE Way*, New York: McGraw-Hill, 1999.

Taylor, Mark, "The 5 Reasons Why Most Projects Fail—And What Steps You Can Take to Prevent It," 2002, http://www.shippingsys.com.

Tenner, Arthur R. and Irving J. DeToro, *Process Redesign: The Implementation Guide for Managers*, Upper Saddle River, N.J.: Prentice Hall, 2000.

Waxer, Charles, "Top Ten Six Sigma Black Belt Candidate Qualifications," 2005, http://www.isixsigma.com/library/content/c030317a.asp.

Index

About the Author

Penelope Przekop is director of Global Quality Management for the Benefit-Risk Management organization within the Johnson & Johnson Medicines and Nutritionals Group. She is a popular guest speaker for groups including the International Quality and Productivity Center and the Center for Pharmaceutical Training.